Rose Blennerhassett, Lucy Sleeman

Adventures in Mashonaland

Rose Blennerhassett, Lucy Sleeman

Adventures in Mashonaland

ISBN/EAN: 9783337178918

Printed in Europe, USA, Canada, Australia, Japan

Cover: Foto ©Andreas Hilbeck / pixelio.de

More available books at **www.hansebooks.com**

ADVENTURES IN MASHONALAND

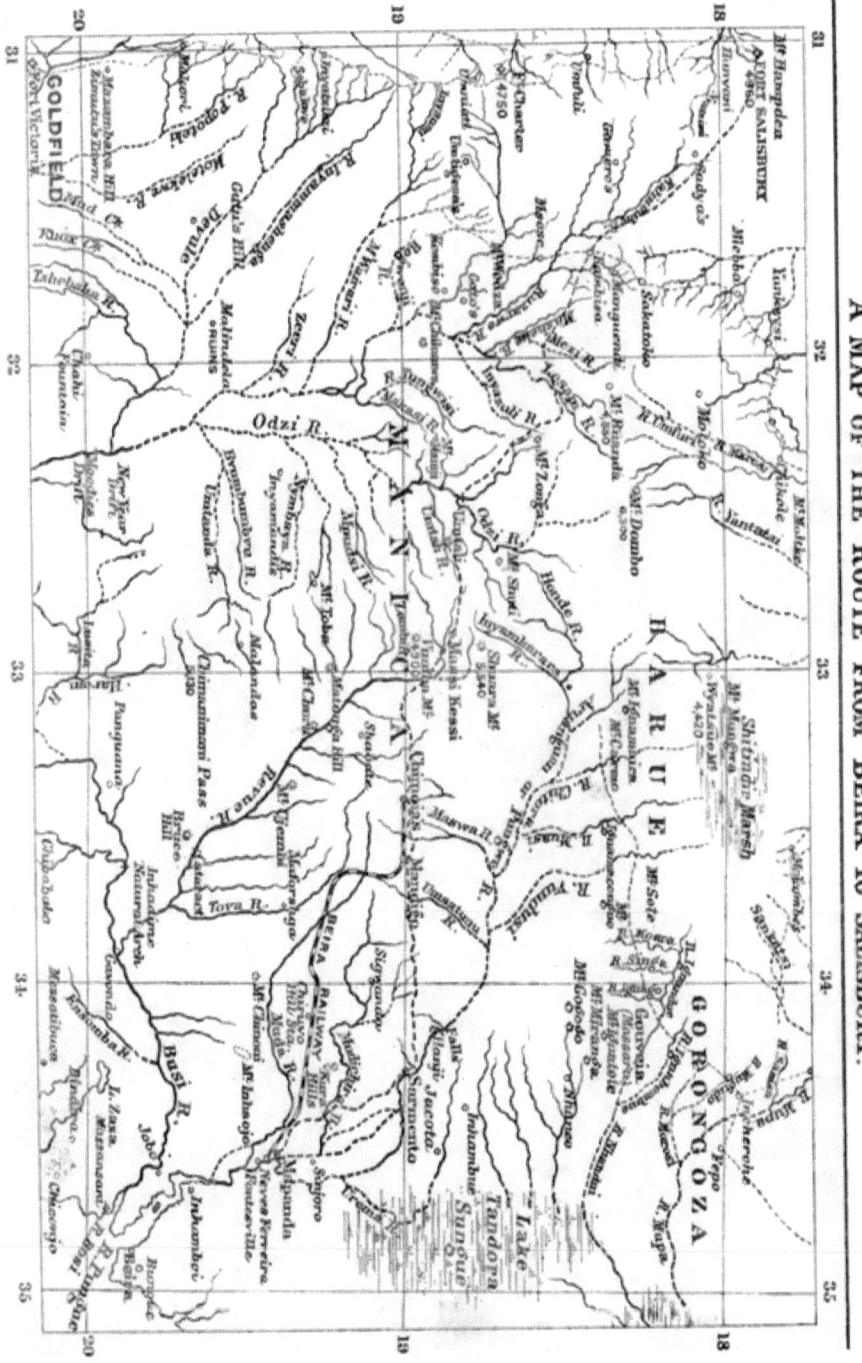

ADVENTURES
IN
MASHONALAND

BY

TWO HOSPITAL NURSES

ROSE BLENNERHASSETT
AND
LUCY SLEEMAN

London
MACMILLAN AND CO.
AND NEW YORK
1893

All rights reserved

To

SEYMOUR-FORT

AND OUR OTHER FRIENDS

IN AFRICA

CONTENTS

CHAPTER I

Preliminary—How I became a nurse—Workhouse Infirmaries—Infirmary Nursing Association—Cardiff Union Hospital—Sad state of things—Reforms—Dr. Sheen—Night nursing begun—House surgeon—Health gives way—Typhoid at Johannesburg—English nurses going out—I join them—Sister Lucy Sleeman—From Natal to Johannesburg—Life in the "Golden City"—Impecuniosity—Life in the Home—A ball—Visit to a gold-mine—We leave for Kimberley—The coach—A drunken neighbour—Kimberley—The hospital—The diamond mines—De Beers compound—Precautions against diamond stealing—Night duty—We propose returning to England . . . . . . Page 1

CHAPTER II

Leave Kimberley—Hear of Bishop Knight Bruce—Offer to go to Mashonaland—Tickets to England—Miss the train—A day outside Kimberley—Bishop's telegram—Off to Cape Town—Meet Bishop—Settle to join Mission—Leave the *Roslyn Castle*—Mr. Maund—Decide to go *viâ* Pûngwé—Plans changed—Stop at Durban—Canon Booth—Indian Mission—Bishop off to Maritzburg—Lodging hunting—Durban and its inhabitants—Visit to house of Jamieson—Mosquitoes—Kaffir huts—Indian service—Bishop returns—Leaves for Beira without us

—"Major" Johnson—Dr. Doyle Glanville—Off at last—Fellow-passengers—Inhambane—The Queen's health—Beira—Fighting up country—Battle of Chua—H.M.S. *Magicienne*—Johnson again—Captain Ewing to the rescue—Off to Mozambique—Mr. Grant's natives—Quilimane—Curios—Beira again . . . . . . Page 25

CHAPTER III

On the Pûngwé—Sixteen hours in the *Shark*—Hippopotami—Crocodiles—Intense heat—'Mpanda's—Nowhere to sleep—Lions—Old Wilkins—Dr. Todd of the *Magicienne*—Fever—Work among the natives—Camp life—The Consul—A plague of rats—Arrival of Dr. Glanville—News from the Bishop—Disputes among Mission workers—Livingstonian anecdote—Sir John Willoughby and monkey-nuts—Collapse of transport—We must walk one hundred and ninety miles—Opposition—The enemy routed—The Portuguese commandante—A Portuguese military hospital—Departure of Consul—Wilkins in search of bearers—His dramatic return—No money—Lieut. Robertson to the rescue 83

CHAPTER IV

The start—A "dug-out"—Missing load—A kraal—Native funeral—On the road—Another kraal—Lions—A Portuguese breakfast—No water—Captain Winslow—We meet two white men—Honey-birds—Lions again—Sarmento—A native hunt—Trouble with carriers—Forced march—Masse-Kesse—We lose our way—Illness of Sister Aimée—At last Umtali—The Bishop 119

CHAPTER V

Sabi Ophir—Illness of Dr. Glanville—Dr. Lichfield—Lieutenant

Eustace Fiennes—No boots—High prices—Maquaniqua the queen—Arrival of Mr. Sutton—Holy Communion—Captain Heany—Sad death of Dr. Glanville—Site of the Mission farm—Appearance of Colonel Pennefather . Page 146

CHAPTER VI

Settling down at Sabi Ophir—Difficulties of cooking—No luggage—Gold panning—Mr. Sutton leaves the Bishop—Description of our huts—Visit from a hyæna—Arrival of Mrs. Tulloch and children—The question of food—Flowers—Mr. Selous visits Umtali—Mr. Teal devoured by a lion—The native labour question—Evils of drink—Our boxes are rifled by the natives—Our first patient—The Administrator arrives at Umtali—Hospital hut opened—Bishop leaves for England—Horrors of night duty—Arrival of Mr. Rhodes—Site of camp moved—The rains begin—Mr. and Mrs. Bent . 165

CHAPTER VII

Leaving Old for New Umtali—Our Malay boy Jonosso—"Your Excellency's plate"—Rain—Waiting for the waggon—An accident—Water-tight huts—Furnishing the hospital—Sister Lucy as carpenter—The white prisoner—His thumbs tied—Algernon Caulfield makes an arm-chair—Illness and departure of Eustace Fiennes—Sister B. Welby and Dr. Lichfield—Arrival of our clergyman—His strange attire—His disputes with the Mission workers—He "chucks his orders"—Advent of a professional baker—Sister Lucy's cake—Its effect on Col. Pennefather—Wedding cake—The first marriage in Manica—Keeping Christmas—The police deputation—The cow—Sports—Magistrate and Civil Commissioner "on the burst"—All the police arrest each other—The last man—General amnesty—The Colonel again—"Order of the Sack"—Good-byes 198

CHAPTER VIII

The hospital—Patients—Work—Contrivances—Project of brick hospital—Poultry yard—Capricious hens—Mashona cows—The bread question—Our baker—Attempts to bake himself—A breadless community—Montague Bowden—His last game of cricket—His illness and death—Scaring off wild beasts—The funeral—Our dispenser "on the burst"—Opium poisoning—Dispenser attempts suicide—Imprisoned—Our protest—Dispenser dismissed—Illness of Sister Lucy—Flight of natives—A terrible week—Drink—An extraordinary bill—Departure of magistrate—The reign of Law in Manica—Birth of first English child in Mashonaland—Serious illness of Mrs. Tulloch—Our huts burnt to the ground—Narrow escape of Mrs. Tulloch—A tipsy fire brigade—Generosity—Arrival of Dr. Matthew Johnston—Our patient saved—Christening of Cecil Rhodes Tulloch—He leaves the hospital in triumph

Page 216

CHAPTER IX

A free day—A visit to Chiconga—Climbing a kopje—The kraal—Gungunyama's raids—The council hut—The chieftainess and her "warriors"—Her answer to the Bishop—We trade—Fashion amongst natives—A blind Lovelace—Instance of ferocity—Kissing—Intelligent children—Absence of religious notions—Differences of language—Ancient gold workings—Worship of Isis—Mosaic Law—Small-pox—Inoculation—Native vanity—Inferior iron-work—Carved snuff-boxes—Fire-sticks—Principal food—Produce—Curious calabashes—Disgusting reports—Chiconga's return visit—A chief's assegai—A demand for fire-water—A Woman's Rights argument—The royal baby—An endless visit—Jonosso to the rescue—The Queen retires 239

CHAPTER X

A tale of horror—" Smelling out witches "—Maronka—His prisoner—An expedition to rescue him—The encampment—Lions—Native carried off—Half devoured—Horses attacked—Night of terror—A plucky terrier—The dead lioness—Maronka submits—Mr. Carden—Home again—Another lion story—Vogler—Besieged by lions—A terrible situation—No water—Rescued—Too late—Vogler's death—More lions—Siege of Umtali—Warlike funeral—Night alarm—A reign of terror—Township attacked—Tracked to his lair—The dead monarch—Lying in state—At peace once more . . Page 257

CHAPTER XI

A luxury—Mr. Seymour-Fort—An eccentric drive—A luncheon party—China *versus* tin—Ill-behaved guests—Moonlight—Our carriage and pair—" Pills and Powders "—Their friendship with our monkey—Warned of a snake—An execution—Dr. Johnston departs—No doctor—A patient from Masse-Kesse—Clark and Paget—Amusing notes—The doctor at last—A *cause célèbre*—Troublesome results—What's in a name?—Gold finds—The gold fever—Wonderful reefs—The Queen of Sheba's kingdom . . . 279

CHAPTER XII

The hospital empty at last—An expedition proposed—We trek to the Odzani—A picnic—Our camp by the " Slippery Drift "—The march to M'Tassa's kraal—A wearisome delay—The King appears—A noisy palaver—Offering a present—Kaffir beer—The King is photographed—Bushman drawings—Return home—Cattle stealing—A warlike expedition—The " Artillery " borrow our donkey harness—An awful old woman

Return of the expedition—News of the Bishop's return—Nurses to relieve us—The Beira Railway—The Jesuit Mission—Splendid organisation . . . . Page 294

CHAPTER XIII

Illness—Visit from a leopard—Tedious convalescence—Again without a doctor—Arrival of the Bishop—New nurses on the way—Their arrival at Umtali—A split in the camp—A touching deputation—Farewell to Umtali—Fever *en route*—In the train—Fontesvilla—Arrival at Beira—A transformation—Lieutenant Hussey-Walsh—Hospitality—The Consul's ball
314

CHAPTER XIV

We leave Beira—On board the German steamer *Kaiser*—Dar-es-Salaam—Evangelical Mission—Mission hospital—Emin Pasha's daughter, Ferida—A madman on board—His strange diet—"We can't lock up an Englishman!"—His death—Zanzibar—The English Mission—Splendid organisation—The hospital—On board H.M.S. *Raleigh*—Bishop Smythies—Aden—The Red Sea—Untimely sausages—Mr. Wolf, the German explorer—Port Said—Europe at last . 327

CHAPTER I

Preliminary—How I became a nurse—Workhouse Infirmaries—Infirmary Nursing Association—Cardiff Union Hospital—Sad state of things—Reforms—Dr. Sheen—Night nursing begun — House surgeon — Health gives way — Typhoid at Johannesburg — English nurses going out—I join them—Sister Lucy Sleeman—From Natal to Johannesburg—Life in the "Golden City"—Impecuniosity—Life in the Home—A ball—Visit to a gold-mine—We leave for Kimberley—The coach — A drunken neighbour — Kimberley — The hospital—The diamond mines—De Beers compound—Precautions against diamond stealing—Night duty—We propose returning to England.

THE unexpected always happens, and nothing happens but the unexpected!

If anyone had told me, ten years beforehand, that the year 1890 would find me a nurse, tending the sick in the heart of Africa, I should have laughed the predictor to scorn. Of all unlikely fates that might befall one, that seemed the most improbable. And a very trivial incident decided the event.

In a village near which I often stayed was an old man suffering from cancer. I used to go and see him. On the occasion of one of these visits I met the doctor, and asked if the old fellow would not be better cared for in the Workhouse Infirmary? Thereupon the doctor enlightened me as to the condition of the neighbouring Union Infirmary, pouring forth a sad tale of untrained nursing, bad food, neglect, and sometimes ill-treatment. He had done what he could; had represented matters to the guardians, and had written to the Government Inspector, but all to no purpose. The infirmary cost little, and economy was the first consideration. Humanity came a long way after.

Just then a report of the "Workhouse Infirmary Association" fell into my hands. This Association aimed at supplying Union Infirmaries with trained nurses. Its report echoed the doctor's tale of neglect.

In a very few days my resolution was

taken. I would be a nurse, and work for the Association, and when I had once made up my mind it did not take long to carry my resolution into effect.

After a medical and surgical training, I went through a course of midwifery, a knowledge of which is essential in workhouse nursing, and, when I had obtained the London Obstetrical Society's diploma, I applied to the Association, stating that I wished to work in a country workhouse. A few weeks later I went as superintendent nurse to the Cardiff Union Hospital.

It is not my intention to write here about workhouse infirmaries. I will briefly state that the Cardiff guardians were exceptionally humane, and even liberal; and that the "master" was enlightened and interested in the hospital. Yet the arrangements for nursing the sick were incredibly bad. I had charge of between three and four hundred beds. My nurses were untrained; there were no night-nurses. Typhoids, covered with bed sores, were left at night to the care of an old woman from the "house." Pneumonia cases, and unfortunates in the last stages of phthisis, had to look after themselves. The first time I went round with the doctor, he said, "Begin with the children's ward, it smells like the den of a wild beast!" Yet Dr. Sheen had already improved the place very much indeed.

The moment I, as a trained nurse, caused the urgent want of a night-nurse to be laid before the Board, they supplied the deficiency. Untrained attendants, however praiseworthy, cannot well judge of what is a real want, and what can be done without. Even if their judgment is good it carries no weight.

Sixteen months later Cardiff Hospital had a staff of trained nurses. The guardians had resolved to appoint a resident house surgeon. The sick were well cared for. Dr. Sheen would long before have carried out these reforms, if he had had any trained nurses to work with him. I count him among my best friends.

About this time my health began to break

down, and I was advised to try a change of work. Hearing that an epidemic of typhoid was ravaging Johannesburg, and that several trained nurses were going out to establish a Nurses' Home there, I resolved to join them. Four of these ladies left in January 1890. I and one more were to start in the spring.

March, therefore, saw me hurrying to Lisbon *via* Paris. I was a bad sailor, and wished to avoid the terrible bay.

Rain and storm pursued me, however, and on one of the wildest days that yet permitted a boat to leave the shore, I embarked for Africa on the Union S.S. *Spartan*. The other nurse had sailed from Southampton, and we met on board. Her name was Lucy Sleeman. We have been together ever since, and have lived through many strange experiences.

After an uneventful voyage we landed at Durban, Natal, of which we saw nothing, having to hasten on to our destination. In those days the journey could only be accomplished by a twelve hours' railway journey, and about sixty hours in a coach. The drive from Ladysmith, where the railway ended, to the border of the Orange Free State was lovely. The road wound up through lofty mountain ranges, and the air was deliciously pure and fresh. Then followed a long monotonous journey across the Free State, mile after mile of the same burnt-up veldt. We nurses rejoiced indeed when the roofs of the "Golden City" glittered in the afternoon sun. They were not golden roofs—far from it! Some were made of corrugated iron, some of biscuit tins. But the effect was good, and the sight welcome. It all meant a bath and a bed, two luxuries from which we had been severed since we left Natal.

A pretty little nurse in a neat grey cloak and bonnet met us at the coach office. She looked fagged, and told us she had just recovered from typhoid. We found afterwards that an undue share of nursing had fallen to her lot. She slaved like a little heroine amongst the typhoids, and the good order which reigned in the little Home Hospital was almost solely due to her exertions. Her name was Sister Janet Hickman.

The Home itself was far from a desirable place. Sister Lucy Sleeman soon went out to a case. For five weeks she nursed a typhoid, in a four-roomed house in which nine people lived! The men of the house used to return home about five P.M., and generally went straight to bed. For a long time Sister Lucy could not understand the reason of this unusual arrangement, but finally discovered that they were almost always tipsy. In those days the Johannesburgher was usually tipsy towards evening. The "boom" was over, business was at a standstill. Thousands of people were utterly ruined, and many men drank to drown care. Very few then believed that Johannesburg would ever again recover itself, but it is now as flourishing as in the best days of the famous "boom."

And what an amazing place it is! In less

than two years a large city sprang up on the bare veldt. True, some of the houses were eccentric. When we were there in 1890 there were still houses built solely of biscuit tins, with Huntley and Palmer's labels clinging here and there. But there was also a stately street of stone buildings, as well as a fine Exchange. The suburb of Dornfontein, with its well-built houses and villas, had already united itself to the town. There were hotels, clubs, public ballrooms, and concert rooms. And, best of all, there was a theatre, where the "gods" made the best part of the entertainment with their amusing comments on audience and stage—comments which were delivered in the most unabashed tones, and, as a rule, were taken good-naturedly.

The Johannesburgher is passionately fond of dancing, so the penniless condition of our Home was naturally considered a good excuse for getting up a charity ball.

Over three hundred people went, and a special request was made that the nurses should be represented. Several of them therefore attended. They described the proceedings as eccentric, to say the least. Nearly all the men, who were of course in a large majority, were very tipsy by ten o'clock. Revolving couples cannonaded each other, tumbled down, and could not get up again. A Church of England clergyman played the fiddle in the orchestra. He was attired in the usual swallow-tail; and wore tight black knee breeches, silk stockings, shoes and buckles. The next day his ungrateful flock commented in the papers on the thinness of his legs.

It was indeed a new and strange world—not such a bad one, however. Whatever may be their faults, the Johannesburghers possess two fine virtues in an unusual degree. Enterprise and rare generosity distinguish them from other South African communities. Notwithstanding the general distress they gave lavishly to our Home, but could not save it from bankruptcy.

Our servants, who were only black boys,

were always running away; often there was only one boy to do all the work of both houses. So the sisters and nurses had to do their own cleaning and sweeping in the Home; whilst two of us were in the other house—one cleaning grates, lighting fires, and so on; the other in the kitchen, washing potatoes, and generally tidying up. We endeavoured to make our Kaffir boy, Cornelius Agrippa, clean saucepans. But in a very short time he flung his saucepan down, disappeared into a sort of packing-case house in the garden, and refused to move for at least half an hour. It was amusing cooking our own dinners, some of us being fairly good cooks. In the middle of our dinner the butcher's boy would arrive; he came for his "little cheque." We told him, as usual, that we had no money. This happened regularly every day. He always returned looking quite hopeful. We used to tell him he would be paid in the "week of the four Thursdays." This speech caused him great amusement, but did not damp his ardour.

The Home really was in a dreadful state. We had hoped to make it a nursing centre, and eventually have a large hospital, but it was crippled by a large debt. When we arrived in Johannesburg we found only £5 in the bank. Without money it was only just possible to scramble along as best one could, looking after the few young fellows who were admitted to the Home. We could take in eleven. These boys—they were little more—were supposed to pay fifteen shillings a day; stimulants, doctor's fees, and drugs extra. Of course very few were ever in a position to pay. Instead, they used to supply the Home with boxes of chocolate creams. This, though pleasant, was hardly practical.

Apropos of drugs, we sometimes wondered whether the medical men were in partnership with the chemists. One never saw anything to compare with the patients' prescription boards. They were really curiosities of literature! It was astonishing that any enteric case, swallowing such a quantity of horrible stuff, and changing his medicines nearly every day, should have survived. Yet some of them did recover in spite of the treatment. About twenty per cent died. Of course there were exceptions. Several distinguished doctors were in practice at Johannesburg, but in those days were in a small minority.

Sister Lucy, myself, and two other English nurses, moved heaven and earth to escape from the place. This was not so easy. Distances are enormous in Africa, and the smallest move is very costly. At last, after much correspondence, the doors of Kimberley Hospital were opened to us, and we prepared to leave Johannesburg after a sojourn of less than six months.

Before leaving we drove out to the cemetery, where the husband of a friend of ours lay buried. She was in England, and had begged me to take a few flowers to his grave. What a sad, sad sight it was! There, within a small space, their graves simply numbered, lay hundreds of young Englishmen and a number of young women. I think that not more than two or three of them were past forty when they died. By far the larger number were between twenty and twenty-eight. It was most affecting, too, to see long, long rows of tiny graves, suggestive of such heart-breaking sorrow. The mortality amongst women and children had been terrible. "When I came up here," said a doctor to me, "the women were literally dying like rotten sheep. One never expected to get a confinement safely over." I think we were all glad to turn our backs on that cemetery, feeling grateful surprise that none of our number were to be left behind there.

An interesting visit to a gold-mine occupied our last day in Johannesburg. The "Robinson mine" was then the most flourishing on the Rand. It was lighted by electric light, and its battery was one of the sights of the town. As we alighted from our Cape cart at the door of the manager's house, he courteously welcomed us, and took us to the shaft, down which we were to descend. It looked rather alarming, the darkness was so intense. Where was the electric light? Certainly nowhere at hand. The darkness of the shaft looked actually solid. Mustering up courage, we got into a sort of iron cage with open sides, and, clinging to each other, were let down into the abyss. After descending for a few seconds one feels as if one was going up again. Then one seems to stand still. This is a dreadful sensation. One imagines the cage to be really stationary, and that it will be impossible ever to ascend again. Happily these fancies do not last long. We soon found ourselves at the bottom of the shaft, and stood in a long subterranean passage or gallery, along which a small tramway ran. In the dim distance a tiny lamp gleamed. This was the electric light. It might have been a night light.

Where was the gold? We saw nothing but mud and rock. Greatly to our disappointment we were informed that no gold could be seen. The trucks which natives pushed along the tram-lines were full of quartz. This dirty-looking rubbish was worth immense sums. We wandered through many of these galleries, and at last, not a little wet and muddy, returned to the light of day.

We now proceeded to the battery, a wonderful place.

In an enormous shed rose, one above the other, a succession of platforms. On the topmost platform a long line of steam hammers rose and fell with rhythmical swing and crash. Night and day they crushed the quartz, which, arriving incessantly in trucks, was precipitated into the machines. By-and-by it poured forth from them in a stream of finest powder. This stream was directed on to huge plates covered with mercury, which occupy the second platform. Water continually flows over these plates, washing away the quartz. Gold mingles with the mercury, forming a substance called "amalgam." The lower platforms are occupied by similar plates of mercury, which catch any gold that may have been washed away with the quartz. The residue of the quartz-dust flows away into a sort of swamp. This residue is called "tailings." We were shown a patch of "tailings," and told it was worth £200,000 at least.

The next process is to retort the "amalgam," separating it from the gold. This latter is finally melted, and flows into brick-shaped moulds. We saw there gold bricks worth £2000 each. The assayer also showed us his scales. These were literally adjusted to a hair; for he pulled a hair from his beard and showed us how its weight was accurately measured. In an incredibly short time the slightest inaccuracy in the scales would make an important difference in the gold returns.

The manager offered us a cup of tea, and then took us to see the white men's quarters. These were very comfortable. There was a well-lit messroom, in which the messboys were laying the table, very tidily; a reading-room, and a well-filled library.

One of the employés told us that, with a little common-sense, a man could save from ten to fifteen pounds a month. The higher employés could save much more. The work chiefly consisted in superintending gangs of native boys. A doctor belonging to the mine looked after the sick.

The work seemed pleasanter and better paid than that of clerks in offices at home. Once off duty you were as good as your neighbour. You could go to any of the balls or concerts given in Johannesburg. There were little or no caste divisions. Barmaids and shop girls skipped about at the balls. Why not? The wives of the "upper ten" had many of them been barmaids and shop girls not so very long ago. Besides all this, a lucky find might make any miner a rich man in the twinkling of an eye.

At last the hour of our departure from the "Golden City" struck. The stars were still bright in the heavens as we said good-bye to the Nurses' Home, and hurried through sleeping Johannesburg to catch the Kimberley coach. We were on foot; our luggage had been sent on the day before.

The coach was of the good old-fashioned type, and a great improvement on the springless waggonette which had brought us from Natal. It was somewhat the worse for wear, having been brought in its old age from California. Bret Harte's chivalrous ruffians had probably travelled by it. This appealed to one's imagination, and made one forget its air of dilapidation.

We stowed ourselves away each in a corner. The remaining space was filled by men, none of them very slim, and one enormously fat. When the sun rose the heat and stuffiness may be imagined. We were packed like sardines in a box. The very fat man sat between Sister Lucy and me. He turned out the best of the lot after all, taking great care of our comfort, and spending long hours in the blazing heat and clouds of dust on the top of the coach to give us more room. His name was Ross. We began by thirsting for his blood, and ended by thinking him a capital fellow.

We left Johannesburg with a team of ten

horses. Every hour and a half we halted and changed the team. At every halt the men got out and drank. No wonder! If I had been a man no doubt I should have done the same. But *noblesse oblige!* We were women; therefore we smiled amiably at heat, thirst, cramp, and general discomfort. We declared it wasn't half bad, and privately wished we had never been born. Sister Lucy suffered most. She is tall, and her legs would not fit in anywhere.

The coach, with its outside passengers and its miserable twelve inside, rumbled along, and at three o'clock in the afternoon brought us to a quaint little Dutch village called Potscherfstrom. Here we rested and refreshed ourselves for an hour. Then on again till eight, when we reached another village. Here we remained till two o'clock in the morning, resting meanwhile on some very dubious-looking beds. Away then through cool moonlight and blazing day, doing close on twenty hours with only an hour's rest. Sister Lucy got outside in the moonlight, and drove us into Christiana at a rattling pace, the last team of horses being in first-rate form. We reached Christiana at half-past ten at night, and were conducted to two small outhouses. Sister Lucy and I took one, the other two nurses the other. The place was unspeakably dirty. We spread our rugs over the beds and lay down.

At one end of the room a thin muslin curtain hung over an opening in the wall apparently leading to a large cupboard. Towards three in the morning we were awakened by a great noise in the yard outside. Strange yells and scraps of songs were followed by scuffling and the sound of a heavy fall, apparently in the cupboard next our room—then silence. We dozed a little. Then I said, "It must be nearly five." To our horror a tipsy voice answered from the other side of the muslin curtain, "Notsh fivesh, foursh; foursh, I tellsh you." There was another entrance to the cupboard, which was a small room, and the noisy tipsy man had been pushed in there!

We fled madly to the other nurses, and were very glad indeed to be whirled away in the coach without our tipsy neighbour. In a few hours we reached a railway station, and a train quickly carried us to Kimberley.

The Hospital is rather a rambling place. The part devoted to European patients, nurses' dining-room, kitchen, and offices, formed a long low bungalow set in the midst of pleasant grounds. Close at hand, but scattered irregularly over a large compound, were the native wards—surgical, medical, women, and lock—each at some distance from the other. The nurses' home was a building apart. The nurses' rooms were built round a flowery quadrangle. Each nurse possessed a little cell, which opened on a shady verandah, or "stoep," as it is called in Africa.

Setting aside the nursing work, I believe that few hospitals in London could compete successfully with the commissariat of Kimberley Hospital. The seclusion and austere respectability of this institution afforded a welcome change after the shiftless scramble of the Johannesburg Home.

Kimberley was the African "Golconda," just as Johannesburg was the "Golden City." Therefore as soon as our work permitted we paid a visit to the De Beers diamond mine. Warned, however, by our underground experiences at the Robinson mine, we refused to leave the light of day. We saw countless numbers of trucks full of blue clay, in which the diamonds are imbedded. Then there are the rooms where the diamonds are sorted. Unusual specimens are kept on show. But we thought nothing so interesting as the great compound.

This is a wide space within a great stockade about twelve feet high. Strong wire netting was fastened above, so that it looked like a monstrous aviary. Here the natives who work in the mines live, to the number of I am afraid to say how many hundreds. They engage to work in the mine for a term of months, agreeing to remain prisoners for that period. They sleep in sheds round the compound, have shops where they can buy what they choose, and dens where they smoke a sort of narcotic plant—in its effects not unlike Indian hemp. All these precautions are taken to prevent the diamonds from being stolen. But for the wire the men would throw the stones over the stockade. As it is they contrive to steal some. The difficulty is to get their spoil out of the compound. A day or two before their time expires they are carefully searched. Strong medicines are also administered in case they should have swallowed a diamond.

A native, however, is very cunning. Some of them have been known to push their stolen stones carefully into a cleft in the stockade. When dismissed, they idle about on the veldt outside the compound, and gradually scratch the jewels out. This process is so difficult and dangerous that the losses of the Company are few, considering the large number of miners employed by them. Notwithstanding their imprisonment the natives seemed very jolly. Some of them were fine-looking men, of a higher type than the multitude. We heard that great chiefs in the interior sent their "indunas," or headmen, sometimes their own sons, to work in the mine in order that they might steal diamonds for them.

We remained six months at Kimberley, and then the work began to tell on me. I was the night superintendent, and had to go from ward to ward in all weathers. I was often wet through, and of course had to remain wet until morning. The compound was large and unlit. Here and there were large holes, which after rain were filled with water. Into these holes one invariably stumbled when in a hurry. Apart from this, continuous night duty does not suit all constitutions.

After consulting together, Sister Lucy and I agreed to go home together, and looked forward to enjoying an English summer. We little dreamt at that time that we were destined to remain two years longer in Africa. Instead of being at the end, we were scarcely at the beginning of our African experiences.

CHAPTER II

Leave Kimberley—Hear of Bishop Knight Bruce—Offer to go to Mashonaland—Tickets to England—Miss the train—A day outside Kimberley—Bishop's telegram—Off to Cape Town—Meet Bishop—Settle to join Mission — Leave the *Roslyn Castle*— Mr. Maund—Decide to go *via* Pûngwé — Plans changed — Stop at Durban—Canon Booth—Indian Mission—Bishop off to Maritzburg—Lodging hunting—Durban and its inhabitants—Visit to house of Jamieson—Mosquitoes—Kaffir huts—Indian service—Bishop returns—Leaves for Beira without us—" Major" Johnson—Dr. Doyle Glanville—Off at last—Fellow-passengers—Inhambane—The Queen's health — Beira—Fighting up country—Battle of Chua—H.M.S. *Magicienne*—Johnson again — Captain Ewing to the rescue—Off to Mozambique—Mr. Grant's natives—Quilimane—Curios—Beira again.

IN the spring of 1891, therefore, Sister Lucy Sleeman and I were getting ready for our homeward journey, and expecting to be back in England in a few weeks. At that time the Chartered Company's expedition to Mashonaland was in everyone's mouth. A concession had been obtained from Lobengula, the great Matabele chief, and pioneers and police were in the heart of the country.

Wonderful reports came from Mashonaland to the colony. We heard of grass ten feet high, of trees sixty feet in circumference, of mysterious ruins. The whole country was said to be one vast gold-reef. But the way from Cape Town to Mashonaland was long and perilous. Swamps, which exhaled poisonous vapours, had to be traversed. Swollen rivers, swarming with crocodiles, had to be crossed. Boats and canoes were not to be procured, the men were forced to swim across. Oxen fell sick, and died by the score on the long trek. Fever ravaged the pioneers.

Under these circumstances the Company were endeavouring to make a new and shorter route to the interior. For this purpose steamers were to run from Durban to the Pûngwé—a large river between Mozambique and Delagoa Bay. At the mouth of it was a small Portuguese station called

Beira. It was supposed that the Pûngwé would be navigable for nearly one hundred miles, and that a road from thence to Fort Salisbury, the capital of Mashonaland, could be easily made.

The Chartered Company had seized Manica, or South-East Mashonaland. This territory was claimed by Portugal, but not much importance was attached to the claim. M'Tassa, the native king of Manica, had given a concession to the Chartered Company. Everyone in Kimberley was either going himself to Mashonaland, *viâ* the Pûngwé, or had a friend or relation going up; and when it became known in the Hospital that the Bishop of Bloemfontein had given up this diocese for that of Mashonaland, considerable interest was aroused.

In a short time we were told that Dr. Knight Bruce wished to take nurses up to his new diocese, where he projected establishing several hospitals. However, the Mission the Bishop was organising was poor. The hospital scheme appeared likely to fall through for want of funds. It seemed a pity. After some discussion with other nurses, Sister Lucy Sleeman and I volunteered to go with Dr. Knight Bruce. A third nurse offered to accompany us if the Mission could pay her £40 a year. This was, considering the undertaking, a nominal salary, but circumstances forbade her going without any remuneration at all. After some delay the Bishop's answer came. He said we were mistaken in supposing that his hospital project had failed. He thanked us for our offer, but all his arrangements were completed. I can honestly say I was much relieved, and took our passages to England with unalloyed pleasure.

The morning of our departure came, and we set off in the highest spirits.

But our adieus had been too prolonged. As we reached the station we just caught a glimpse of our train puffing out of it. There was not another to be had for twenty-four hours. Lamentations were futile. We left our luggage at the station and drove out to a house, half inn, half farm, where we could lunch and while away the time till evening.

The inn was not unpicturesquely situated in the midst of the dreary desert plain that surrounds Kimberley. A few good-sized trees afforded shade. A small stream of water trickled over great granite boulders, falling with a pleasant splash into a pool. As we sat after luncheon beside this pool, I remember saying that Africa was a difficult place to escape from. It was like a huge devil-fish. Once it caught you, escape was impossible. For my part I felt as if we should never get away. My companions laughed at the notion. They said our tickets to England were like amulets, and would break the evil spell. Unless we missed a train every day for a week we could not miss our ship. In spite of these excellent arguments events proved that I was right, and I cling to the belief that for once I had a real presentiment.

On our way back to our Kimberley hotel

we called at the post-office to see if any letters had arrived for us. There fate overtook us in the shape of a telegram from the Bishop, asking us to join him. I urged a refusal. "He who will not when he may, when he will he shall have nay," seemed to me the spirit in which to answer. Finally a compromise was effected, and we telegraphed to say we would meet Dr. Knight Bruce at Cape Town, and consider the possibility of accepting his proposals.

The Bishop, in fact, appeared at Poole's Hotel, Cape Town, the day after our arrival. We found him comparatively young for a Bishop, not much past forty, very pleasant and persuasive, and with an exceptional talent for getting out of a room well—a much rarer gift this than one might suppose. The Bishop's exits were always effective; he evanesced rather than went, always at the right moment, and left behind him a little hush, in which one would place a note of admiration.

We told him we had heard that his plans

were somewhat indefinite. On this point he reassured us. He said that in the disturbed state of Mashonaland and Manica, with the Portuguese question coming to a crisis, a cut and dried plan of action was impossible. He wished to go to Port Beira and up the Pûngwé, and thence by waggon to Salisbury, where fever was rife. He could not feel sure whether we should manage an hospital established by the Mission, or the Company's hospital; he believed the latter. This perhaps sounded somewhat indefinite. He had engaged a first-rate doctor, who was daily expected; he had his builder, a man who had been with Livingstone; his carpenter, and others. A clergyman and some other young missionaries would take his waggon up by the long trek, from Cape Town or Natal, to Salisbury. The Bishop had his own medical stores; the Company had large stores already up there. We should require to think of nothing but a personal outfit. We told him that though we were not at all "fine," and were quite ready to do anything that might want doing, as far as we could, yet we were unsuited physically for such work as "daghering" huts or "smearing floors"—that is, plastering walls with a mixture of mud, water, straw, and cowdung; and smoothing a sort of liquid manure over floors, which hardens, and can be swept and kept clean. We had heard at Kimberley that "daghering" and "smearing" would be essential parts of our work.

Dr. Knight Bruce again reassured us on this point, saying there would not be any such rough work, as it would all be done by natives. We should have a white cook and orderly, at least for the first year. He had been a ship's steward, and we should find him most useful. Later on we could make other arrangements according to circumstances. These points being settled, the Bishop asked us to engage ourselves to the Mission for one year; but, after some discussion, in which we pointed out to him that it would be impossible to do much towards establishing an hospital in one year, it was settled that we should give our services for two years, and that the Mission should pay our passages back to England at the end of that time.

The next few days were one continual rush and hurry to get an outfit in time. It was of great interest to us to see our tent, a charming marquee, and think of living in it; and to note all the preparations for a real campaign in the interior of Africa. By the 16th of April, 1891, our purchases were made, and we embarked in the *Roslyn Castle*, *en route* for the Pûngwé. This river, as yet unexplored, and sometimes known as the Aruangua, was said to be navigable for small steamers, at least as far as seventy miles from its mouth at Beira. It was proposed to take the pioneers this distance up the river; establish a camp for the storing of goods; and convey them by waggon and coaches, drawn by trotting bullocks, as far as Salisbury, a distance of about four hundred miles. A Road Company had been formed for this purpose, the road being supposed to be already completed.

The Bishop having decided on going to

Port Elizabeth by train and joining us there, we were taken on board our steamer by the well-known Mr. Maund. This charming traveller had already gone up to Mashonaland by the inland trek, immediately after the first pioneers had opened up the country; had visited Lobengula, the great Matabele King; and had had the honour of taking his indunas to England, and presenting them to the Queen. He told us that Gordon Pasha had been one of his dearest friends, and that illness alone had prevented him from making his way to Khartoum. Mr. Maund impressed us as being one of those delightful people who invariably secure the best cabins in ships, and the best boxes at the play, and have the best appliances in every emergency. He gave us some useful information about modes of life up country, predicting our safe arrival there *viâ* the Pûngwé, in spite of the Portuguese difficulty. Questioned as to this, he said it might be briefly summed up as a dispute between Portugal and the British South Africa Company about the possession of Manica, or South-East Mashonaland. He supposed that the Portuguese had been the first to explore that province, but they had not colonised it, nor had they any concessions from the existing chiefs. If they had, Mr. Rhodes would "square it." We afterwards found this to be a sort of watchword in Africa. Whatever happens, people shrug their shoulders and say : " It will be all right, Rhodes will square it."

After a pleasant dinner Mr. Maund went on shore, and the *Roslyn* steamed majestically out to sea. On the 18th of April we arrived at Port Elizabeth, one of the most uninteresting, colourless towns it is possible to imagine, though I believe the country round about is beautiful, and from some of the heights near the town we caught exquisite glimpses of sea and distant hills. We had to wait at this wearisome place till Monday evening. The Bishop arrived just at dark, and the bay was so rough that there was some difficulty about getting him on board. Hardly was this effected when the anchor was raised, and we soon saw the lights of Port Elizabeth disappear in the distance.

Next day the Bishop told us there was really no chance of our being able to go to Beira and up the Pûngwé. Sir John Willoughby and some of the Company's people had been fired at by the Portuguese, and were obliged to return to Natal. We should go by train from Natal to Maritzburg, and thence by post-cart and waggon to our destination.

This was disappointing; we had looked forward to travelling by an entirely new route, and had heard great things of the Pûngwé as a beautiful river on whose banks lions stood and roared, but always at a safe distance. However there appeared to be no help for it, so we resigned ourselves to the inevitable.

On Wednesday the 22nd we reached Durban. The long line of green, monotonous coast had not prepared us for anything so beautiful. Indeed we were delighted with Durban. The bay is dotted with islands and picturesque mangrove growths, whilst the wooded heights of Berea form a lovely background to the town.

We nurses went to the Royal Hotel, where all the service is done by Indians, swathed in muslin and bare-footed, and giving a charming suggestion of Orientalism. The Bishop was put up by Canon Booth, doctor and missionary, one of the most interesting people it has been my fortune to meet in Africa.

The next day we had to unpack everything, and repack in the smallest possible compass for post-cart travelling. We were to start for Maritzburg at three in the afternoon. At one the Bishop came and said we could not leave till next day. I told him I had a presentiment that we should go by the Pûngwé after all; and, although he said this was quite impossible, still it appeared to me that very probably the Willoughby incident would bring matters to a crisis. And as the Portuguese were hardly likely to embark on a war with England, the result would be an understanding between England and

Portugal, and the route to Manica would be thrown open.

As if to justify my presentiment, the Bishop came to us on the 24th, and told us that our places were taken in train and coach, but that he had given up the land route, and was going to make a push for the Pûngwé after all. The reason of this complete change of front was that he had met a man who had just arrived from Mashonaland, and said that he had left there last December. He had been four months on the journey, and described the routes as in a terrible state, owing to the worst rainy season that had been known for many years. Many trekkers, he said, had been forced to abandon their waggons on the banks of impassable rivers. So it appeared to be better to wait at Durban until the Pûngwé route was open.

A certain Johnson had obtained a contract for transport from Beira to Mashonaland, and had formed a Road Company. There was a pioneer camp on the Pûngwé called

'Mpanda's, and from there the Road Company's waggons were to start. A road was in process of construction, and nearly finished. A fast coach would also run from 'Mpanda's to Salisbury, by which we could reach the latter place in ten days.

In spite of the prospect of a tedious delay at Durban, we rejoiced over this plan, and hoped it would prove more stable than the others. That same afternoon, however, we had another visit from the Bishop. He came to tell us that he thought it useless to wait, and that we must be ready to start for Beira next morning in the *Venice*. He believed that by the time we reached the Pûngwé the Portuguese difficulty would be disposed of. We hastened to make all the needful arrangements, and it was a great disappointment when the Bishop reappeared that same evening, and said he thought it would be better to let the *Venice* go without us. She would touch at several ports and take ten days to get to Beira. The *Norseman* would go in eight or ten days' time, reaching Beira in four days. The Bishop intended spending the interval at Maritzburg, and proposed to take us there also, leaving us with a sisterhood, whilst he stayed with the Governor. By this time we were much bewildered by the constant changes of plan, and began to think we should never arrive anywhere. We were, therefore, not much surprised when the next morning he suggested our staying at Durban, instead of going to Maritzburg with him.

The hotel being very dear, Canon Booth's sister kindly called for us to go lodging hunting.

Our first experience was a strange one. We went by tram to the top of the Berea heights, catching most exquisite glimpses of the town and bay. We stopped at a boarding house which was said to be extremely "refined and elegant." The cream of the shipping-agency clerks would there find "home comforts and intellectual conversation" for a moderate price. The mistress of this abode received us in a tea gown, in the midst of a confusion of antimacassars, scent bottles, fans, and all sorts of odds and ends. She allowed us to see a very dirty room next a stable, in which a coloured man was sleeping, and told us we must keep a light burning all night on account of the swarms of rats. She thought we could all sleep in it "somehow," and was much shocked to find that, although we were "nursing sisters," we did not think this accommodation sufficient. But we felt that we should have unavoidable opportunities for mortifying the flesh later on, and that it would, therefore, be useless to make ourselves uncomfortable on purpose. So, saying good-bye to the presiding genius, we set out in search of something cleaner, if less intellectual; and were fortunate enough to discover a dear, simple Scotchwoman, by name Miss Wright, who had a background of brooms and dusters, instead of fans and scent bottles. Here we established ourselves that very evening.

The next day was Sunday, remarkable

only for one of the longest, weariest, and dullest sermons it has ever been my fate to endure, which we heard at St. Cyprian's, the most important church in Durban. A walk home by the exquisite moonlight somewhat compensated for the hour and a half in the hot, stuffy church. The effect of light and shade, as we passed along an avenue of feathery bamboos was indescribable, a thing to feel and dream about.

Our uniforms attracted a good deal of attention, quiet as they were—the cross which the Bishop wished us to wear making them more conspicuous than they otherwise would have been. The fact, too, that we were bound for Mashonaland made us objects of general and very kindly interest. Everyone who had the slightest acquaintance with our hostess called, and requested her to bring us to call.

Some of these ladies had most charming houses, built here and there along the Berea heights. We were specially delighted with the house of a Mrs. Ballance, a fascinating old lady, still extremely handsome, with a quiet, dignified manner—a refreshing change after the somewhat emphatic colonial cordiality. From the terrace of her house we looked down on a waving mass of tree tops. In the middle distance, sweeping in long curves round the bay, the white houses of Durban glittered in the evening sunlight. The bay itself lay absolutely still—not a ripple breaking its vivid blue-green colour; whilst the distant shipping out in the open, with here and there a glint of foaming breakers, gave animation to the scene.

One's first impression at Durban is that one can never leave it again, and that life in the midst of its dreamy beauty must be ideal. But after a few days one realises that it is always the same view—a beautiful but monotonous effect of light and colour; and one longs for barren and rocky shores.

Possibly the plague of mosquitoes has some influence in breaking the spell. Sister Lucy Sleeman and I appeared to be small-pox patients. We were literally swollen out of all resemblance to human beings. The mosquito curtain indeed protected us somewhat at night, but the insatiable mosquitoes devoured us all day long. We were told that an excellent remedy was to burn Keating's powder on a shovel. We did so, but only succeeded in giving ourselves violent headaches, accompanied by vomiting and general discomfort; whilst the mosquitoes went to sleep for an hour or two, and woke up like giants refreshed.

The British South Africa's agent at Durban, Mr. Jamieson, asked us to go to his house at Bellair, about twenty minutes by train from Durban. So we set out one morning, and arriving at the Bellair station, found Mrs. Jamieson there to meet us. She was most kind and cordial. The house, surrounded by a lovely garden, commanded fine inland views of wooded hills and undulating plains. We were glad to lose sight of the perpetual sea view. The garden, which we explored after luncheon, was filled with every sort of strange flowering shrub and tree, collected from all parts of Africa. Mrs. Jamieson was devoted to her garden; each plant seemed to be a special friend, and to receive special care, with the happiest results. A hedge of martinguelas—at that time partly covered with fruit and partly with its white starlike blossoms, which exhale a strong perfume, something like that of a gardenia —shut off the garden from some Kaffir huts, built exactly like the native hut, untouched by civilisation. We crept into one of them, and examined its beehive shape and smooth, hard, earthen floor with much interest, as huts like these would probably be our home for the next year at least. On the whole we concluded that it was odd, but not half bad, and that it would be possible to make a patient tolerably comfortable in such a surrounding. We did not return to Durban till late that evening.

On Saturday, the 2nd of May, the Bishop returned to Durban, and preached at St. Cyprian's on the following Sunday. In the afternoon we all went down to St. Aiden's, the church of the Indian Mission. Few things at Durban are more interesting than this Mission. Canon Booth, who is its founder, was at one time a doctor practising in India. Taking orders, and settling at Durban, he has devoted his life, energies, and fortune to the services of the Indians of Durban. A large room—half study, half surgery—is attached to the group of church and schools, and here the Canon looks after the physical well-being of his flock. The service was conducted in an Indian dialect, and a very intelligent-looking Indian deacon preached.

The language did not strike us as being harmonious, but the gestures of the preacher were so graphic, and his features so animated, that it was really possible to get at the drift of his sermon. The singing was monotonous and barbaric beyond expectation. Poor as the church was, its very poverty appealed to one's imagination more than do many more splendid churches. The Indian women, delightfully draped in many coloured stuffs, looked like so many Old Testament illustrations, and suggested a shadowy background of palm-tree, desert, and camel.

After service we had a sort of picnic tea in the surgery. The Canon outside his work is as full of fun as a boy, as, indeed, most "all round" men are, and we amused ourselves very well, till the fading light reminded us that it was time to get back home.

We had a long talk with the Bishop next day. It was settled that we were to go with him by the *Norseman* on the 6th of May. He looked very fit, and was in excellent spirits, having enjoyed himself much at Maritzburg. Of course we rejoiced greatly at the near prospect of leaving. We expected to reach Beira in three or four days, and to find the waggons and coaches of Johnson's Road Company at 'Mpanda's, seventy miles up the river. Our hostess on the Berea declared herself very sorry to lose us. She, however, entered into the spirit of our venture, and procured us lessons in bread-making. Sister B. Welby, who was with us, and who knew something of baking in the ordinary way, went to some people who were accustomed to trek over the veldt, and was initiated in the mysteries of bread-making in an iron pot, over an open-air fire. Unfortunately her experience was not of much use to us. She left us a few months after, as will appear later on.

The long waited for Wednesday dawned at last, but, alas! the *Norseman* was not ready. She would sail the next day. It seemed to our impatient fancy that these delays would never end. To occupy ourselves we went to see the Durban Hospital. We were much shocked by its dirty, disorderly wards. Dirty dressings were lying about, clothes lay on the floor near the beds, the nurses were invisible, and an atmosphere of complicated unpleasantness seemed to pervade the whole place. No doubt all this has long since been reformed. We heard that there had been many complaints about the hospital, and no wonder. No one interested in hospital work could see such a place without a feeling of intense depression. But I write of over two years ago, and since then I hear that Lady Mitchell's trained nurses have given nursing in Natal an impetus in the right direction.

Thursday, the 7th of May, was a sadly eventful day. We were up betimes, and sent our luggage down to the boat. We were to follow towards midday. But at half-past nine in the morning we received a hurried summons from the Bishop, requesting us to join him as soon as possible at the Royal Hotel, where we should meet Mr. Johnson, the manager of the Road Company.

Full of unpleasant presentiments, Sister Lucy Sleeman and I hurried to the hotel, the third sister declaring herself unequal to the interview. Arrived at the hotel, we found the Bishop alone, and seemingly much disturbed. He said he feared we could not go with him, that he must go alone, and that we should be able to follow in about a month!

I cannot describe the despair we felt at

this announcement. We must have shown very great discouragement, for the Bishop begged us not to allow our very natural disappointment to damp our zeal for the work. He said he had discussed the matter exhaustively with Mr. Johnson, and we should see this person ourselves, and hear all he had to say.

Mr. or "Major" Johnson, as he elected to call himself, then appeared. He was a dark, somewhat stout man; seemingly good-natured; and with a rather noisy, jovial manner, which probably does him good service in the many unpleasant emergencies which a habit of romancing on all occasions necessarily create in the long-run,—withal, I believe, a staunch friend and a man of exceeding energy.

He made the following statement, which proved to be so entirely without foundation, that if it had not been written in my Diary within an hour of its having been made, I should feel it impossible to believe that I had heard it:—

"The officer in charge of the road-making department in Mashonaland," he said, "has indeed made his road, but, unfortunately, he has directed his road to a river seventy miles south of the Pûngwé, instead of taking it to the Pûngwé as directed. This river is called the Sabe. It has therefore been necessary to cut a road through one hundred miles of bush, in order to unite the Pûngwé to the existing road, the additional twenty miles being caused by the swamps, which it is needful to avoid." Major Johnson then proceeded to say that if we went up with the *Norseman* we should have to spend ten days on the Pûngwé in an open lighter, crowded with white men and with natives, who were to be engaged in road-making. He said there was really no accommodation for women, and that the swampy nature of the banks of the Pûngwé would make it impossible for us to have our tent pitched and live on shore.

Of course, disappointed as we were, it was impossible not to see that if we insisted on going with the *Norseman*, we should not only be useless, but a trouble and hindrance, and should find ourselves in an altogether impossible position. So, having to yield, we did it with the best grace we could muster. Major Johnson and the Bishop hoped that we might perhaps be able to get away on the 16th of May. They assured us that when we got to Beira we should find a small steamer, the *Agnes*, ready to take us up to the pioneer camp, where the waggons would be in readiness, and a considerable portion of the road finished. The Bishop's doctor—Dr. Doyle Glanville—who was daily expected, would travel with us.

Dr. Knight Bruce seemed somewhat depressed by the continual obstacles which cropped up unceasingly. He said he counted on our "cheery courage," and of course we were very anxious to make as few difficulties as possible. Still the prospect of being left behind, we three women, to make our way into the interior with an entirely unknown man, could not fail to make us feel anxious and troubled. By way of raising our spirits, too, Major Johnson told us that the whole country was in a state of convulsion; that "rebel" Portuguese troops defied the control of the Governor of Mozambique, and persisted in attacking the English; and that fighting was expected beyond Masse-Kesse. In point of fact, the Portuguese troops were not at all mutinous; no news of a *modus vivendi* had penetrated into the interior, and Portuguese and English were preparing to fight in earnest. It is not altogether surprising that, as we saw the *Norseman* steam away, we felt very forlorn indeed, and I think a few futile tears were shed.

Day after day slipped by in monotonous succession. From time to time rumours of fighting up country reached us, and on all sides we were assailed by entreaties to return home, and give up an attempt which would prove fruitless. In the shops the people who served us with a biscuit or a yard of ribbon would ask if we really meant to go to Mashonaland, and advise us not to do so.

Often we were stopped by women, who would say with tears, "Sister, my son (or brother) is up in Mashonaland—take care of him if you meet him." An old man in a tram-car was so pathetic over our future fate, that Sister Lucy was beginning to be quite touched, when our friend suddenly lurched forwards and fell under the seat. We then discovered that he was extremely tipsy, and were very much ashamed of having listened to him. One evening, as all three of us were taking a constitutional outside Durban, some old people, who were driving a sort of gig, stopped and asked us if we were really off to Mashonaland. They seemed to think we were starting then and there — walking off without escort or luggage! We reassured them with some difficulty, and explained that, when we did leave, it would be very comfortably in a steamer.

On the 15th of May Dr. Doyle Glanville appeared. He was a tall, soldierly-looking man, past his prime, with a very important manner, but seemingly not a bad fellow *au fond.* To our great consternation he said that he knew nothing of any settled plan of the Bishop's; that he was bound to the Union Steamship Company, being a doctor on board one of their steamers; and that it would be quite three weeks before he could start up country. He thought we must decide for ourselves whether we would wait for him, or go on and try to catch the Bishop at 'Mpanda's. For himself, he had to hurry back to his ship.

This left us in a state of trouble and perplexity easily to be imagined. The next day we received a letter from the Bishop from Beira, telling us that he expected us by the next steamer. We heard on all sides that it was more than probable we should reach 'Mpanda's before the Bishop could leave, as it was said that the troubles in Manica were taking very serious proportions, and that the road-making party had been forced to leave off work, and return to 'Mpanda's. Still it was rather an important step to take, and we resolved to consult Colonel W——; Mr.

Watts, the Union Company's agent; Mr. Jamieson, the agent both of the Chartered Company and of the Bishop; and others. All of them advised us not to wait for the Doctor, but to make a push for 'Mpanda's. One of the Bishop's people, a boy called Wilson, had remained behind with us, and would, we thought, be a sufficient protection. He was a youth from the east end of London, exceedingly sharp and useful, able to put his hand to most things, but apparently not very strong. He, too, was consulted, and elected to go with us.

On Wednesday, the 28th of May, we said good-bye to our kind hostess, turned our backs on Durban, and steamed forth into the unknown on board the coasting steamer *Tyrian* commanded by Captain Morton. The vessel was crowded with men — Pûngwé pioneers—some going up as traders, all more or less as prospectors. They were full of hope and enthusiasm about the new country; nothing was heard in the ship but a perpetual talk of "booms," "reefs," "alluvial," and of all the chances there appeared to be of making a rapid fortune.

Amongst our fellow-passengers was Mr. Grant, son of the famous explorer, on his way to Mozambique, where he intended to engage a number of carriers, to take up the Zambesi to the Lake Country and beyond into the interior. He was a very pleasant young fellow, who had already done a good deal of exploring work, and with whom it was very interesting to talk.

Mr. Walter Sutton, the ill-fated son of the archdeacon of that name, was with us too, the picture of health. He has since disappeared on the veldt up country, and there is little or no hope of his ever being seen again. Many another of our fellow-passengers has since joined that ever increasing majority. The greater number of the others we were to meet again under very different circumstances.

Captain Morton told us that he did not see how Dr. Doyle Glanville could possibly follow us till nearly the end of June, so it really seemed as if we had been well advised in not waiting for him.

Passing dismal, fever-stricken Delagoa Bay and Lorenzo Marques, we reached Inhambane on Saturday, the 23rd. We could not land that evening, but spent it on deck watching a total eclipse of the moon, and admiring our surroundings. The town or rather village of Inhambane was of considerable importance in the palmy days of the slave trade. A large, stone slave market looked quite important from the sea, but on closer inspection proved to be falling into ruin. There were large stone houses also, quite out of keeping with the present proportions of the place. Here for the first time we made acquaintance with the beautiful feathery cocoa-nut palm, groves of which fringe the bay, and cover the many islands reflected in its clear still waters.

The following day we went on shore, and were almost instantaneously mobbed by natives. Apparently these had never seen European women before, for they followed us, to the number of forty or fifty, wherever we went, evidently criticising freely—and, probably, not always favourably.

Those houses which were inhabited were chiefly of the wattle and daub order, spotlessly clean, and built in the midst of large shady compounds. In spite of the heat we strolled beyond the village, through groves of cocoa-nut trees, and, coming to a small native hut, asked Mr. Grant to send a boy up one of the palms to bring us some nuts. This he did. The boy forthwith picked up a hatchet, and, cutting little holes in the tree as he climbed, inserted one big toe after another into the holes, and was soon at the top of this improvised staircase, squatting comfortably among the nuts and branches, or rather branching leaves. He threw down some fine nuts, which his father opened for us. It being the 24th of May, we drank the Queen's health in cocoa-nut milk. Our attendant crowd of natives had never left us, and solemnly watched us imbibing the milk, but Sister Lucy, who didn't like it, made a grimace at them, upon which they shrieked with joy, throwing themselves on the ground, and rolling about in an ecstasy of enjoyment. As we walked back to the ship we met other natives, who were informed of the great joke, and they in their turn attached themselves to us. At last, however, the noise became so intolerable, to say nothing of the heat and smell, that the white men were obliged to threaten our bodyguard with their sticks, whereupon the whole crowd fled, making for the beach, where they awaited our advent, and gave us a last yell as we rowed back to the ship.

On Tuesday, the 26th of May, we reached the much-talked of Port Beira. There was considerable difficulty in getting into the harbour owing to shoals and sand-banks, and to this day, in spite of buoys and charts, ships continually go aground. Captain Morton, however, was both skilful and lucky; and though he had never before entered this harbour he did not make a single mistake, and we anchored safely opposite the "town."

This said town of Beira may be described as a long flat reach of sand, over which a few tents were scattered. There were also two iron shanties, and that was all. The place looked, even from afar, the picture of desolation.

The harbour, on the contrary, was extremely animated. As we cast anchor, H.M.S. *Brisk* steamed out to sea, H.M.S. *Magicienne* and the gunboat *Pigeon* being anchored not far from us. One or two beautiful little Portuguese gunboats lay at a little distance; boats flitted from ship to ship. Presently Captain Pipon of the *Magicienne*, Acting-Consul at Beira, came on board the *Tyrian*. Captain Morton introduced him to us, and we found him very cordial and kind. The news he gave us was bad. He said that the Chartered Company's people and the Portuguese had fought at Masse-Kesse, the latter being driven from the fort, which was occupied by the English.

It was rumoured that troops of disbanded Portuguese soldiers were roaming about the country, revenging themselves on all English-speaking folk whom they might come across. Colonel Machado, Governor-General of Mozambique, had therefore declared the route to Fort Salisbury to be closed, since he could not be responsible for the safety of anyone attempting to pass through Portuguese territory; and Captain Pipon had come to request Captain Morton to put up a notice informing his passengers that whoever attempted to go up the Pûngwé did it at his own risk and peril, and must not expect British protection if he got into trouble.

Afterwards we discovered that all these rumours had reached Beira in a very garbled condition. It was indeed true that there had been fighting at Masse-Kesse. Captain Heyman, of the Chartered Company's Police, having been ordered by the Portuguese commandante at Masse-Kesse to leave Manica, or he would be driven out, promptly marched from Umtali to Masse-Kesse with forty-five men and a seven-pounder, took up a good position near that fort, and by dint of sending up rockets and making signals, impressed the enemy with the idea that he was only reconnoitring for a large force. This force, of course, was absolutely mythical, he being hundreds of miles from any possible help. By-and-by provisions ran short with the gallant forty-five. Spies informed them that there were at least five hundred men in Masse-Kesse, and a large supply of "thunder and lightning," as natives call artillery. Action of some kind was imperative. As Captain Heyman was debating the possibility of an attack by surprise, the enemy, much to his gratification, marched out of the fort and proceeded to attack him.

The Portuguese troops were nearly all coloured men, either natives or half-caste. They did not fight well, and after one or two futile attempts to storm the English camp, they all ran away. No artillery was used by the storming party. Twice the European Portuguese officers, who are said to have behaved splendidly, tried to rally their men, beating them with the flats of their swords; but, finding it futile, they all three walked slowly away at a more than funeral pace. Two or three volleys were fired at them, bullets ploughing up the earth round them. It was found afterwards that one, I think Monsieur de Bettincourt, was wounded in the neck rather badly, and another in the arm. They made no sign, however, until, just as a rising ground was about to hide them from view, they turned, took off their hats to the English, and strolled slowly back to the fort. Convinced that a large force must be behind Captain Heyman, Masse-Kesse surrendered. The Company's people found stores of food and medicine, and I believe artillery, to the value of ten or twelve thousand pounds. Captain Heyman says that if the commander had been equal to his position and resources, not an Englishman ought to have left Manica to tell the tale. Of course Captain Heyman, by his pluck and readiness of resource, really secured Manica to the Company. This is in substance what occurred at the "Battle of Chua," as it is called. It took place on the 11th of May, 1891. It is needless to say that the anniversary is always kept in Manica with much feasting and many speeches. I tell the tale, as it was told to me by the "heroes of Masse-Kesse" and others, with but little variation, though as I did not reach Umtali till two months later, I may possibly be wrong in some of the details. Everyone knows how difficult it is to repeat with absolute correctness.

To return to Beira. We had expected to find a small steamer called the *Agnes* to take us up the Pûngwé. We were quite resolved to go as far as 'Mpanda's, where, as the route was closed, the Bishop was in all probability to be found. He was said to have bought a piece of ground at a little distance from the pioneer camp, and to have pitched his tents on it. We heard in the evening that the *Agnes* would probably appear next day.

The next day arrived, but no *Agnes* was to be seen. Captain Pipon asked us to lunch on board the *Magicienne*. We went, and enjoyed ourselves very much. He took great trouble to show us everything of interest in the ship, and explained the torpedo arrangements so wonderfully, that, for the space of a flash of lightning, I knew how to handle torpedoes; what use to make of them; how to manage a ship; and a great many astonishing things which now are hazy as a dream.

The *Magicienne* struck us as being a beautiful, but perhaps not very comfortable, ship. The engine-rooms took up an immense space, and the accommodation of the crew seemed to be of little importance. Electric bells, springs, lights, and appliances abounded on board; every shelf and cupboard did something offensive or defensive, if required. The kitchens seemed to be as perfect as the engine-rooms. An excellent luncheon was sent out of them, and altogether we found Captain Pipon capital company.

A rumour now reached us that the Bishop had left 'Mpanda's with a Portuguese called

Captain da Silva, and four natives. This made us still more anxious to get on, and we hoped the *Agnes* would arrive on Friday at latest. We heard that she was aground on a sand-bank in the Pûngwé, and that this was the cause of the delay. We had three cases of fever on board, but none of them were serious.

Meanwhile the pioneers on board the *Tyrian* became very impatient indeed. The next morning they all came on deck in true stage freebooter costume — rifles, knives, long boots, truculent-looking hats, cartridge belts, nothing was wanting. They announced their intention of capturing Beira forthwith, and set off to interview Captain Pipon on the subject. What happened—whether they saw him, and if so what he said—I never heard, or do not remember. I know, however, that Beira was not captured, and I think it was a great pity. It is now becoming quite an important place. Two-thirds of the inhabitants are English, and I do not think that Portuguese rule suits them, or tends to develope the resources of the place, which is really forced along, in spite of obstacles, by the English element.

The capture of Beira having fallen through, more peaceful plans prevailed, and we went to a concert on board the *Pigeon*, where we spent a very pleasant evening. Scarcely had we got back to the *Tyrian*, when a storm broke out; the harbour became so rough that the decks of the *Pigeon* were completely under water; and if we had been ten minutes longer aboard of her, we should have been unable to leave at all till next day. We expected to make the acquaintance of Mr. Jerram, acting captain of the *Pigeon* later on, as he was for the moment Vice-Consul at 'Mpanda's. Captain Winslow of the *Brisk* was also up country.

Neither Friday nor Saturday brought the *Agnes* or any news of her. The weather was so rough and cold that we could not go on board the *Magicienne*, where a concert had been got up to amuse us. It was indeed weary waiting. Beira was dirty, and, the anti-English feeling being naturally so strong, Captain Pipon requested us not to go on shore.

However, the *Agnes* really did appear on Sunday morning, with Major Johnson on board her, and a few minutes after she had cast anchor he was rowed over to the *Tyrian*. Our first inquiries were for the Bishop, and we were indeed sorry to hear the news of his departure from 'Mpanda's confirmed. Major Johnson said that the Bishop and da Silva had lost their way, and; after walking about thirty miles, before they discovered that they were going towards the coast instead of towards the interior; had both returned to 'Mpanda's. As the Bishop is an experienced traveller and sportsman, we concluded that this must have been da Silva's fault, as it in fact proved to have been. He professed to know the country, and undertook to guide the party, happily with no more disastrous result than a waste of about two days' time on a useless and tiring march. On their return to 'Mpanda's, da Silva objected to go any farther, and the Bishop was said to have pushed on ahead with only one boy, other bearers having refused to go. There was said to be considerable difficulty about obtaining native labour, the natives waiting to see which were to gain the day, English or Portuguese, and fearing to compromise themselves with either party. After a good deal of talk, Major Johnson told us that we could not possibly go to 'Mpanda's at that time. He did not see how he was to get us up the Pûngwé. The *Agnes* would have to take the pioneers, and would be crowded with men; it would be impossible for three women to go up with that crush. Also the *Agnes* would take two days going up, if she were lucky and did not run aground, in which case she might be a week.

Captain Morton and Johnson advised us to go with the *Tyrian* to Mozambique; with the understanding that, on her return to Beira, we should have the *Agnes* to ourselves, and go up the river in her. Feeling that we could not trust to these promises—so often made and always broken—we were about to decide that we would be landed at Beira, and make our way up for ourselves, even if that course involved going in native "dug-outs," when a new adviser appeared on the scene.

This was Captain Ewing, owner of a little Thames launch called the *Shark*. In appearance somewhat like the pictures of Don Quixote, he was a man who had been almost everywhere, had done almost everything, and was universally liked. What was more to the point, he was said to be strictly a man of his word. He is now Port Captain at Beira.

Captain Ewing advised us to go on to Mozambique, saying that the 'Mpanda-Salisbury road had not progressed at all, owing to the Portuguese troubles, and that the road-making parties had been obliged to return, and were forbidden by the Portuguese commandante on the Pûngwé to leave the pioneer camp. The Bishop alone had been allowed to proceed on his journey.

We should gain nothing by going to 'Mpanda's, but should be only shut up there for at least a month. So he strongly urged our remaining with the *Tyrian*, and gave his word of honour that, if the *Agnes* failed us on our return to Beira, he would himself take us to 'Mpanda's in his *Shark*. It was very bitter to us to have come so far, and to have actually reached Beira only to meet with another long delay. But, though quite determined to fulfil our promise to the Bishop, and get to Mashonaland by hook or by crook, we were particularly anxious to do nothing headstrong or unreasonable. We felt also that, dependent as we were on the goodwill of all these men, we should be more likely to obtain both help and sympathy by showing that we were amenable to honest advice. Of course many of them urged us to "chuck the Bishop," as they expressed it, and return to England. But this was not to be thought of. The Mission had gone to great expense in the purchase of stores, tents, etc. The Mission doctor was hurrying on behind us, and the Bishop had gone up country in the full conviction that we were following as fast as possible. No one could hold him responsible for the troubles which had arisen, and the unforeseen difficulties which had cropped up. Africa is the land of the unforeseen. The best-laid plans are unexpectedly swept away in the twinkling of an eye by a native raid, an unprecedented flood, a "boom" in some hitherto unheard of place, to which everyone rushes, "chucking" everything and everybody, regardless of every previous promise or engagement. A will-o'-the-wisp is more steady than the African political horizon. "Questions," "wars," "difficulties," spring up at an instant's notice. There, too, where the most experienced experts and geologists had declared it to be impossible to find gold, are now the richest gold-fields perhaps in the world. Yes, that "nothing happens but the unexpected" is indeed the motto of Africa.

Doubtless it would have better pleased

the Bishop if a steam-tug had been ready for us at Beira, and a fast coach at 'Mpanda's. It would, therefore, have been unfair to blame him for the collapse of the Road Company and for the other difficulties which had sprung up in our way. Of course, in our secret souls, we felt that it would have been wiser if he had remained at Durban till we could all start together for Beira. But he probably thought that it would be for everyone's advantage that he should go on first, and have huts and hospital ready for us when we got up. We must believe, therefore, that he acted for the best.

Inevitable Fate then decreed that we should wander on to Mozambique, from which place it would be impossible to get back to Beira till the 11th of June. That evening an unfortunate white man, whom the *Agnes* had discovered lying in an unconscious and half-starved condition in an open boat on the Pûngwé, was brought on board the *Tyrian*, Dr. de Burgh taking charge of him. He was very ill indeed all the next day, and we fed him by teaspoonsfull every quarter of an hour, night and day.

On the 2nd of June we left Beira for Mozambique. Our sick man was a shade better, but still very bad. Sisters Lucy Sleeman and B. Welby were utterly prostrated by sea-sickness. I was not very bad, so stayed with the patient; but what with the smell of his food, the stuffiness of his cabin, and one thing or another, I soon began to be sick also, and had the curious experience of trying to nurse a bad case in the intervals of all the qualms of sea-sickness. I held on for a couple of hours, and then was forced to call a steward and give up my place to him. Nothing takes pluck out of one like sea-sickness. The spirit felt angry and ashamed, but the flesh was triumphant and collapsed.

The *Tyrian* went straight to Mozambique, where we arrived on the 4th of June. The very picturesque old town is built on a small island. The houses are large, built of stone; and are painted pink, blue, green, and every colour of the rainbow. A massive old grey fort, built in the sixteenth century, I think, lends a certain air of dignity and calm to the somewhat confused and gimcrack brilliancy of the modern town. The light plumes of the cocoa-nut palms wave above the house-tops; boats flit over the bay; Arab dhows, all sail and no hull, fly along like monstrous birds; great steamers puff noisily out to sea. Whilst we admired the lovely, animated scene, our ship was suddenly besieged by a fleet of native "dug-outs" filled with fruit, coral, shells, or fish. We bought some lovely shells, but the coral was white, and looked brittle and cumbersome, and did not tempt us. We had great amusement out of the native fleet of canoes, which were either dug out of the trunk of a tree or made of bark. They were very ricketty, it being generally impossible for a man to stand up in them without upsetting. One native paddles the canoe, another squats at the bottom, and scoops out the water all the time. If the water gets the better of the scooper, both men jump overboard, turn the canoe upside down to get rid of the water, right her, and start again.

The next day we went on shore, hoping to find some curious specimens of native work, which we could take home. We found nothing, however, but the very commonest English goods — coarse shirts of staring colours which the "sweated" must have turned out for "sweaters" by the hundred at home; frightful earthenware dishes; and things of that sort. We admired the Mozambique women swathed in graceful if scanty drapery, and walking, as I suppose none but an African or an Indian woman can walk, with the perfection of grace.

The Governor's house, the barracks, and the hospital, were quite splendid, or looked so in their surroundings. Such buildings would be better suited to Durban or Cape Town than to Mozambique, a sleepy hamlet, the commerce of which is, I hear, slowly but surely drifting away to other ports—to Beira,

I believe, among others. I suppose the decline of the slave trade has ruined these once flourishing towns.

The following day was Saturday, and Mr. Grant's natives to the number of seventy-nine came on board. Such a chattering amusing crowd, draped in every imaginable colour, swarming up the ship's sides like monkeys, pushing each other into the water, and laughing perpetually! Mr. Grant did not intend to take another white man with him, but proposed to go quite alone. He said a companion was a nuisance, as the climate is so irritating that it is impossible not to squabble, and one is always having rows about nothing particular.

We reached Quilimane on Sunday evening; but, the tide not permitting us to go up the river, we had to stay in the open till the next morning. Mr. Grant's natives never seemed to sleep. They danced, sang, laughed, or told stories, like those that Mr. Mounteney Jephson has written about, and were not quiet for an hour, night or day.

The parrot-house at the Zoo would have been a place to retire to for peaceful meditation, when compared with the Union S.S. *Tyrian* after the invasion of Mr. Grant's natives. The night we spent outside Quilimane they made an especially terrible noise, for they had eaten a week's provision of rice in one day, and Mr. Grant having refused to give them any more, they screamed, and danced, and told stories with even more than usual energy—to drown care, or, perhaps, with an eye to digestion.

We got rid of them next day, when we steamed up the river and anchored opposite the town of Quilimane, a pretty-looking place buried in trees, but I should think very unhealthy. We went on shore as soon as possible. It was always delightful to escape from the ship, which was so crowded that there was very little room to walk about. We should, indeed, have been uncomfortable had not Captain Morton, with thoughtful kindness, made us free of his chart-house, which we used as a little sitting-room.

Quilimane is composed of well-built stone houses, standing on either side of wide roads, and surrounded by gardens. The orange trees were laden with fruit, and there were pine-apples and banana trees flourishing everywhere in all the wild luxuriance of African growth. The shops were just like those of Mozambique, and very disappointing. Quilimane is only about fourteen days from Bombay, and the Arab dhows are constantly going backwards and forwards, yet we could not obtain a single Indian rug, a piece of Indian silk, or any of the beguiling trifles which India exports. The shops both at Quilimane and Mozambique were much like East-end stalls. The most important of them sold English soap, which we were glad to pounce upon.

We made the acquaintance of the Acting Consul, Mr. Belcher, with whom Mr. Grant was going to stay. He took us for a long walk through the picturesque woods that surround Quilimane, and procured us some curios — such as gold beads made out of

Zambesi alluvial, and long chains of marvellous fineness, like those of Venetian workmanship, which the natives beat out of a sovereign. If one has time, it is interesting to give a sovereign to the worker and see a chain evolved out of it.

We could not leave Quilimane till the 11th of June, and glad we were to be off again, life in the coasting steamer having become most wearisome. We took in a good stock of the oranges for which Quilimane is famous. On Friday, 12th June, we again anchored in the Pûngwé Bay, and Major Johnson once more came on board, having come down from 'Mpanda's. He told us that before leaving it, he had himself seen our tent pitched on the spot chosen by the Bishop, our stretchers put up, and everything made ready for our arrival. Our tent, he said, had been borrowed for some sick Europeans, but they were then convalescent, and no longer needed it. He told us also that Dr. Todd of the *Magicienne* was looking after the sick at 'Mpanda's, the

Company's doctor being seriously ill. There had been, Johnson added, a good deal of illness in the camp, but it was all over now. Nearly all this news which he gave us was found, on our arrival at 'Mpanda's, to be altogether misleading. Captain Ewing now appeared on the scene, telling us that the *Shark* would be in readiness at four the next morning, and that we must not keep her waiting, or we should lose the tide. It was essential to get to 'Mpanda's in one day, the little launch having no sleeping accommodation of any sort or kind, and a night amid the thick river fog being a thing to be emphatically avoided. Therefore, very soon after dinner, we went to bed, looking forward immensely to at last saying good-bye to civilisation.

CHAPTER III

On the Pûngwé — Sixteen hours in the *Shark* — Hippopotami — Crocodiles — Intense heat — 'Mpanda's — Nowhere to sleep — Lions — Old Wilkins — Dr. Todd of the *Magicienne* — Fever — Work among the natives — Camp life — The Consul — A plague of rats — Arrival of Dr. Glanville — News from the Bishop — Disputes among Mission workers — Livingstonian anecdote — Sir John Willoughby and monkey-nuts — Collapse of transport — We must walk one hundred and ninety miles — Opposition — The enemy routed — The Portuguese commandante — A Portuguese military hospital — Departure of Consul — Wilkins in search of bearers — His dramatic return — No money — Lieut. Robertson to the rescue.

WE were up betimes on the morning of Saturday the 13th of June, and ready and eager to start in the *Shark*, which steamed up alongside the *Tyrian* punctually at four o'clock. But a thick fog suddenly enveloped us, sweeping down the Pûngwé with magical swiftness, so that we had to curb our impatience and wait till nearly five. The fog then lifting a little, Captain Ewing decided on venturing up the river, as a longer delay meant losing the tide, and having to spend a night in the *Shark*. The little launch being the tiniest of steam-launches, in which we three, Captain Ewing, and two sailors, had barely room to sit, the prospect of a night on board was anything but pleasant.

We started, puffing gaily away, and soon lost sight of the *Tyrian*, picking our way carefully amongst islands, which loomed dimly through the fog. After about an hour and a half the fog lightened, and then we discovered that we had somehow drifted round an island, and were rapidly returning to Beira. No sooner had we altered our course, making some advance up the river, than we stuck on one of the shifting sandbanks, which render the navigation of the Pûngwé so troublesome. To this day, in spite of the many careful charts which have been made, steamers drift on to unexpected shoals, being often detained thus for many hours.

Our sand-bank, however, did not delay us more than half an hour.

By this time the sun had dispelled the mists, and we glided along in our little boat, which looked like a tiny speck on the wide rapid river, able at last to take note of our surroundings. Swift, dark, and mysterious, the broad Pûngwé flows smoothly along, between low flat banks, whose vivid green verdure betrays the swampy nature of the soil. Families of cranes of every conceivable colour stalked about in the shallows, or stood pensively on one leg, giving us an indifferent, supercilious glance as we passed.

Suddenly we heard a crashing amongst the branches and thick vegetation to the right of our boat, and a troop of hippopotami plunged heavily into the water. We took great delight in watching them swimming about, splashing, diving, or floating along like huge logs—although I think we were at first a little afraid, having heard terrible tales of the enraged hippopotamus crunching up boats for pastime as he enjoyed his morning bath. But these were amiable monsters, or perhaps only contemptuous. In any case they took no notice of us. As if in contrast to these great beasts, a number of curious little amphibious creatures, half bird, half reptile, flitted past the launch. We had scarcely finished wondering at them, when a flight of brilliant butterflies crossed the river just over our heads. There must have been many hundreds of them, for we at first thought it was a swarm of locusts. Never before or since have I seen so many butterflies, and I am told it was an unusual sight.

The vivid green that fringes the river only partially conceals long, low mud-banks where monstrous crocodiles sun themselves. One or two, disturbed by our passage, dropped sullenly into the water. They filled us with horror. Out of such evil, glittering eyes might lost spirits and condemned souls look forth. The Pûngwé literally swarms with them.

Now, however, we became indifferent to all

sights and sounds. Noonday was approaching, and the heat was gradually becoming more intense. The launch had no awning; barely a yard separated us from the boiler. The water became a great, glittering, dazzling plane. Our eyes ached, our heads burned. We stood up now and then, that being the only change of position possible. An insatiable thirst consumed us. Even I, whom my friends used to liken to a rabbit, because I never wanted to drink, felt dry and parched; but of course I suffered much less than my two companions. The river water was quite hot; and very nasty and unwholesome on account of the quantity of rank, decaying vegetation over which it flows. It served to fill one's mouth with from time to time, but did not afford much relief. We had a little claret on board and a few oranges; without these latter I don't think we could have got on at all. As it was, there were moments when I felt as if there might be worse fates than that of being eaten by a crocodile. It would at all events be cool at the bottom of the river. We were, however, determined not to grumble. Afterwards Captain Ewing confessed that he had expected us to break down, and give him a "d——d bad time," to use his own forcible language.

Towards four o'clock, a light breeze springing up, life once more became the delightful business it generally is.

In spite of a sand-bank or two, on which we had now and then stuck for a few minutes, we had made good way, and expected to reach 'Mpanda's about six in the evening. The fires had been more than once raked out with tremendous noise, emptying of cinders overboard, and clouds of dust. We were going a good pace when we passed Nevez Fereira, a Portuguese encampment, fifteen miles by river from 'Mpanda's, where the Portuguese soldiers, with beating drums and rifles levelled at us, had obliged us to stop and explain ourselves. Suddenly something went wrong with the screw, we crawled along in a jerky fashion, and took nearly six hours doing fifteen miles. The sun leaped out of the sky into the nether world, as it does in those climes; and the marvellous tropical moonlight shed its clear radiance over the river, leaving the thick bush on either side shrouded in impenetrable darkness and mystery. If that veil of shadow had been lifted what strange monsters would have been revealed—fierce lion, gigantic python! As we could not see, we imagined. By-and-by the moon deserted us, thick mists gathered around us, the screw could no longer force the launch off the shoals. Captain Ewing and his men got overboard, and shoved us off. The agonies of mind we suffered, lest these brave men should be snapped up by a passing crocodile, may be fancied better than described.

It was half-past nine when we reached 'Mpanda's. As soon as the shriek of the *Shark's* steam-whistle was heard, half the camp must have rushed to the landing-place. Lanterns flashed to and fro. A number of men shouted questions, and offered incomprehensible advice. But an authoritative voice silenced the clamour, and directed our launch to go alongside a lighter, across which we might walk to land.

The voice belonged to Mr. Jerram, acting captain of the *Pigeon*, and Vice-Consul at 'Mpanda's. He welcomed us cordially, and sent one of his "pigeons" to make coffee for us. Mr. Dymott, the Road Company's agent, then came forward, and said he was very sorry that there was nothing ready for us. Major Johnson had told him there was no chance of our coming up to 'Mpanda's. Our tent was still occupied by three Europeans who had been ill. He would see how he could put us up in the morning, and meanwhile he placed his tent at our disposal for the night.

This was cold comfort to us poor women, tired out with over sixteen hours in the *Shark*, expecting to find our tent ready for us, and looking forward to a peaceful night. We did not exactly bless the memory of the imaginative Johnson. However, nothing is so futile as grumbling. We accepted the situation with such calm that Mr. Dymott conceived the idea of keeping our tent altogether, a project which Captain Ewing and the Consul frustrated.

Wilkins, the Bishop's builder and headman—an excellent but doddering old person, whom it was amazing to think of as of having been with Livingstone—guided us to Mr. Dymott's tent.

In the midst of its dirt and confusion bed and sleep were out of the question. We curled ourselves up in a heap on one of our waterproof sheets, and waited for day. Now and then we dozed, but were soon aroused by unaccustomed sounds—the long, weird shriek of a hyæna; the roar of a lion. These latter were half a mile off at least, but we thought they were actually in the camp! I think a few tears were shed in that tent; we could not help feeling forlorn, alone, without even an acquaintance, in the midst of these wild surroundings, but were of course resolved that no one should even guess what we felt.

It was scarcely light when Wilkins, followed by his native boy, appeared with coffee, a bath, and a couple of buckets of water, requesting us to come to his tent as soon as we were dressed, when breakfast would be ready.

After we had made a hurried toilet, the native who was squatting outside the tent guided us through the camp to the Bishop's encampment. This, at that time, consisted only of a small tent belonging to Wilkins, and two patrol tents for the carpenters, the natives, and kitchen purposes. A large supply of stores, partly covered with sailcloth, lay in front of the tent. Breakfast was spread on a flat, square packing-case, propped on two other boxes.

During the meal Wilkins told us he had already seen Mr. Dymott, requesting him to let us have our tent immediately. This gentleman had demurred, saying that he would "run us up" a grass hut, or lean-to, adjoining the bar, from which we could very conveniently obtain our meals. "But I knew, sisters," said old Wilkins, "what was doo to females; and I says, Mr. Dymott, I says, if that there tent ain't returned by ten o'clock, I'll strike it over the heads of them that live in it!"

Anxious to avoid a row, we sent a note to the Consul, begging him to have the matter arranged quietly, but saying that if the men who lived in our tent were not convalescent they must of course keep it. Mr. Jerram answered that they were up and about, but had no place to go to, and were not well enough to cook for themselves. He added that women could not possibly live in or near a bar in a pioneer camp, and that it was absolutely necessary for us to have our tent.

He and Captain Ewing asked all the Europeans in camp to volunteer with their natives, and build a hospital hut for the use of any Europeans who might want a shelter. In an incredibly short time the hut was put up, and that afternoon old Wilkins had the satisfaction of pitching our tent near his own.

We, meanwhile, had not been idle. Very soon after breakfast Dr. Todd of the *Magicienne* called, and asked us to help him with his sick. He told us that the Road Company's natives were in a shocking state. Two had been found dead that morning in the miserable shelter—it could not be called a hut—into which they were crowded. Twenty-eight or thirty of these natives had refused to work two days before, saying they were ill. The whites believed they were shamming, therefore no rations were served out till they would go to work. The death of two of the poor creatures gave convincing proof of the reality of their sufferings, and saved the remainder. Dr. Todd refused to attend to them unless proper rations of native meal, with such meat and medical comforts as were available, were served out to them. Of course he had his way,—most determined men have, especially in Africa. Nor were the white men deliberately cruel, rather were they thoughtless and self-absorbed.

Besides which, the home-staying European can form no idea of the powers of aggravation possessed by the natives. Tricky as water-sprites, they rejoice in the confusion their blunders create. A native who upsets his master's soup-pot just as that worthy clamours for dinner, cannot help grinning from ear to ear. Then he gets knocked down, but hardly has he touched the earth when he is up again like an elastic ball, and away he bounds to a group of other boys, who listen to his tale with delighted laughter; and if they are pursued, he and his friends are quickly hidden in the long grass. As the irate white man, giving it up, marches off in search of a dinner, black heads peep out from unexpected places, and splutters of mocking laughter follow him. More than once have we watched such scenes at 'Mpanda's, and it cannot be wondered at if the native is looked upon as a nuisance, impossible either to get rid of or tolerate. In reality he is nothing but a grown-up child, and, if treated as such, loses much of his power to irritate.

Dr. Todd took us through the camp to the native huts. The white men's quarters—tents and grass huts flung down confusedly on the banks of a muddy stream—were squalid and wretched beyond description. The Pûngwé bounded the camp on the right, and a stagnant creek ran along its front. Empty tins and refuse of all sorts strewed the space between the tents and huts. As for the natives, they were crowded into two wretched grass shelters—about twenty-eight sick, and I don't know how many others. We had to go into these huts almost on hands and knees.

The first thing to do was to clean up, and this we did at once, making brooms out of branches of trees. Then we got our patients into tidy rows on mats, blankets, or rags, whatever was available; took their temperatures; fed them; hung a washing book to a nail to do duty for a ward book; and soon established a fair imitation of hospital routine.

Dr. Todd was delightful to work with. Had these miserable natives been his own belongings he could not have done much more for them. They had been engaged by the Road Company at Durban, I think, without much reference to their physical condition—some were phthisical, nearly all weakly.

The work in these huts being somewhat trying on account of heat and smell, and the want of all appliances for cleaning, I undertook it myself, with Sister Lucy Sleeman, whose clever nursing and unselfish devotion to the sick proved so invaluable in every emergency. Sister B. Welby took charge of four Europeans, who were under Dr. Todd's care. One of these, who was suffering from a gun-shot wound, would certainly have lost his arm but for that doctor's timely arrival at at 'Mpanda's.

In two or three days regular food and attention began to tell on our patients, who improved very rapidly. So one afternoon,

Dr. Todd and Mr. Jerram, thinking we were beginning to look fagged, proposed taking us for an hour's row on the Pûngwé, and showing us the road of which we had heard so much. To our astonishment and amusement the "road" making consisted of setting fire to the tall grass, neither more nor less. We lit some of it ourselves, and felt as if we were materially advancing that "opening up of Mashonaland," which was in everyone's mouth.

On our return to 'Mpanda's we found some new arrivals, who told us that Dr. Glanville had left Beira; was on board the *Agnes*, stuck somewhere on a Pûngwé sand-bank; and might be expected at any moment. This was very good news. We had now been some days at 'Mpanda's, and had seen enough to know that coaches and waggons to Salisbury were the least substantial of airy myths. Major Johnson had indeed assured us that the first coach had started for Mashonaland, but had omitted to add that it had arrived nowhere, and was stationary on the veldt not far from the Pûngwé camp, merely serving to carry the provisions of the road-making party. We passed it on our way up, unable to move either backwards or forwards on account of the condition of the fly-stricken oxen, most of which had died.

A prolonged stay on the banks of the Pûngwé was of all things to be avoided. Though Mr. Jerram and Dr. Todd had done so much to reform the sanitary condition of the camp, they could not make it healthy. The stagnant creek sent forth pestilential exhalations; the heat was suffocating; tall, rank grass, and groups of the sinister-looking "fever trees," kept off every breath of air. These "fever trees" are a species of mimosa, with pallid boles and livid green foliage, and the experienced explorer always avoids their neighbourhood. Every night a dense fog from the river closed round us, and was not dispelled till the sun had been up for an hour or two. After the scorching heat, the damp misty nights seemed to chill one to the bone.

Nor was it easy to sleep in spite of the comfortable stretchers which had been provided for us. Our tent, like every other, swarmed with rats. They scrambled up and down the canvas, constantly falling on our beds, and sometimes on our faces. We were all of opinion that the wild beasts outside were much less terrible than the rats! At that time we believed that neither lion nor leopard would venture into a camp. We were destined to be rudely undeceived later on at Umtali.

As far as creature comforts were concerned there was nothing to complain of, indeed the waste and profusion around troubled us not a little. Wilkins, who took great care of us, had no idea of thrift. The white men under him, and even their natives, would attack the great pile of stores at all hours of the day, and stinted themselves in nothing. We resolved to speak to Dr. Glanville as soon as he arrived, and request him to put the whole of our small encampment on rations.

Our first letter from the Bishop amused

us much. It was brought by a "runner," and was tied up in a bit of "limbo," and stuck into a cleft stick. What a much more poetical way of receiving letters than by the English penny post! Not so safe, perhaps—but then even poetry has two sides, a wrong and a right one, if you choose to examine things closely. I remember the Bishop telling us afterwards that, as he travelled up country, he met several natives who attached themselves to his party. One of them had a small dirty bundle dangling from the end of an assegai. This bundle was always falling into swamps, and being fished out of rivers. At last the Bishop asked what it was. It was Her Majesty's mail!

To return to our letter, which did not seem to have suffered much *en route*. The news from up country was bad, though the Bishop had arrived safely at Umtali. He said that there was not the slightest chance of waggons or coaches reaching 'Mpanda's for two months, and it seemed improbable that they could return to Umtali in less than two months more. He thought we might engage bearers, and have ourselves carried up in "machilas"—a sort of hammock slung on a pole.

The state of things in Mashonaland was, he told us, unsatisfactory. The worst rainy season known for years had turned the rivers into impassable torrents. Miles of veldt were nothing but a vast morass. It had been almost impossible to get any provisions up to Fort Salisbury — none had reached Umtali. The Company's Police had been living on pumpkins and ground-nuts, until Masse-Kèsse and its stores had fallen into their hands. These stores were nearly at an end, and starvation was again threatening. The men had suffered a great deal, having no change of clothes, and being obliged to go on duty and stand or ride for hours in soaking rain. Many of them were without boots or shoes. Nothing kept these troops, as perhaps they may be called, together, but the profound conviction that it would all come right. "Rhodes would square it."

I have even heard an excited personage declare that, "Rhodes would square the tsetse fly." In point of fact, I suppose, he really will have "squared" it before long, the Beira and Umtali Railway being now nearly finished.

The day after we received the Bishop's letter two men walked up from the *Agnes*, having been put ashore, and having made their way along the Pûngwé banks. We were disappointed that Dr. Doyle Glanville was not with them, and we sent a note by the *Pigeon*, explaining that it was fairly easy walking, from the spot where the *Agnes* was stuck, to the camp—a distance of from six to eight miles. We also sent the Bishop's letter to him, that he might be prepared for the collapse of the Transport Company.

Not till Wednesday, the 18th of June, did the Doctor arrive in one of the boats of the *Agnes*, leaving that steam-tug, and the lighters she was towing, still fast on the shoal, with no immediate prospect of getting clear of it. At certain times of the year the Pûngwé becomes so low, that only specially built flat-bottomed boats can navigate it comfortably.

Dr. Glanville seemed eager to push on, and proposed sending a runner at once to the neighbouring kraals, or native villages, to see if we could obtain bearers. There were a number of these villages round 'Mpanda's, and we had excited the curiosity of the natives, they having never seen a white woman. As we breakfasted or lunched in our tents, a troop of natives would glide silently up to it, squat in a semicircle close to the opening, and watch us intently. After a few minutes they would retire, and give place to others. Every day the same thing happened. We began to wonder why our meals had a special interest for them, since they did not appear to watch the white men feeding. At last it was explained to us. The natives could not understand our waists, or how we contrived to induce the food to pass our waist-bands. They expected, and probably hoped, that some terrible catastrophe would ensue. I need hardly say that our waists were of the most ordinary work-a-day proportions, that we wore flannel shirts, and were guiltless of stays.

The afternoon of the Doctor's arrival, another letter from the Bishop arrived, repeating what he had said before, and requesting us to go no farther than Umtali. He himself was about to push on to Fort Salisbury in search of provisions, and he begged us to bring as much food-stuff as possible with us.

It being obviously necessary to husband our stores as much as possible, the doctor drew up a scheme of rations, forbidding any one except Wilkins to touch the stores. The result was a great disturbance. The white men attached to the Mission declared that they would neither be "rationed" nor be "under" Wilkins! They had been promised home comforts—you could have jam and butter at the same meal at home, why not in Mashonaland? One of the men left; one retired to his tent like Achilles, and could not be pacified. Little Wilson, our East-ender, took a more reasonable view, and subsided into sullen resignation.

After all, it must be remembered that these white men had been entirely uncontrolled and unrestricted since the Bishop's departure. The authority of old Wilkins was nominal. They were not inclined to accept orders from any one but the Bishop himself. The Doctor did not know how to manage them, and Wilkins himself refused to acknowledge his authority. It was a very uncomfortable phase of our experiences. Dr. Glanville had only been in Africa as part of a great military organization, which moved him here and there like a pawn on a chess-board. He had no idea how to move a pawn himself. He was surprised and non-plussed when the well-to-do colonial men, who made rather a favour of serving the Mission, objected to being treated like "Tommy Atkins." Old Wilkins became a stumbling-block in our way. "Should a man who had been with Livingstone be ordered about like this?"

We sometimes wonder, by-the-by, whether old Wilkins had been with Livingstone, he told us such incredible stories about him. I repeat one of them.

"One morning, sisters, and 'tis as true as I'm a biting this crust, we were surrounded by strange niggers—and them niggers meant mischief if ever a nigger did. Livingstone he says, 'We're lost,' says he; 'we must go back and give up. Come here, Wilkins, and advise me!' And I up and says, 'Give up, Doctor? never! Let's go and drive 'em off.' The Doctor, he looks at me. 'Right you are,' he says; 'lead on, my brave fellow, and I'll follow!' And as true as I'm a living man we slew seventy before breakfast!" Wilkins professed a lordly contempt for the Stanley expedition. "If Stanley'd known his business he'd have had a man like me to manage for him," he was fond of saying. By which it will be seen that Livingstone's man had an excellent opinion of himself, and was not likely to knock under easily to a mere tyro such as Dr. Glanville.

"I'm a man to be trusted," he would say, with an air of great importance; "them there sisters know what to expect. I'm used to the ways of females, and the very night they came I says, 'Sisters! let there be no mistake —I'm a married man!'" This remark amused the Doctor hugely. He took great delight in leading up to it, and making the old man repeat it as often as possible. Poor old Wilkins! Peace be to his ashes! After life's fitful fever, he sleeps tranquilly on the wind-swept summit of a lofty crag in far Manica.

Rumours of a terrible state of things in Mashonaland flew about our camp. It was impossible to say from whence they came, or who originated them. Sir John Willoughby, in the service of the Chartered Company, had repeatedly declared that large stores had been taken to Mashonaland, and were distributed to all the stations through a commissariat department. We were now assured that he had spoken without sufficient foundation for his assertions. This gentleman, by the way, is known in Mashonaland, and indeed throughout Africa, as "Monkey-Nuts," he having on the march ordered six monkey-nuts (or ground-nuts) per man to be served out. A ground-nut is about the size of a beech-nut. Very likely the story is less true than *ben trovato*. I never met Sir John, but, when he was asked to help the hospital, a large cheque reached me by return of post. Other people were not always so prompt.

Be this as it may, it appeared certain that a considerable amount of distress must have prevailed in the interior. Even at 'Mpanda's the situation began to look serious. The traders who had brought up provisions, in the fond persuasion, that they could take them up to Fort Salisbury in a fortnight, had to eat their stores themselves, and sell what they could in driblets from day to day. Carpenters, builders, workmen of all sorts, who had spent their savings on tools and outfits, consumed their provisions at 'Mpanda's. Then, hopeless and ruined, they wandered back to Beira, and demanded help of the Consul, until Captain Pipon had so many of them on his hands that he sent a notice to the Natal and Cape papers warning people not to come up to Beira. But, as the advertisement of the Road Company had not been withdrawn from publication, many still believed in the coaches and waggons. They came up to judge for themselves, to the ruin of health or pocket—often of both.

We had now been ten days at 'Mpanda's, and there appeared no chance of obtaining boys. Our patients were more or less convalescent. The sick men were to be sent to the coast; many of the natives had already left. Dr. Todd and Mr. Jerram expected to be recalled shortly. Both urged us to give up an attempt at going farther on. They declared we had done more than enough to show goodwill and unusual pluck. Would we not be contented with that, and return home? Or, if we could not give up our plans at once, would we at least go back to Beira? The *Pigeon* was at our disposal, and every effort would be made to make us comfortable on board her.

Dr. Todd declared that if we attempted to walk up, it would be at the peril of our lives. No women he had known had ever walked in Africa; even men found it trying, and sometimes died on the way. We told our excellent advisers that we could only die once, and that dying was just as disagreeable in a room as on the veldt. If women had never walked in Africa there was no reason why they should not begin. Supposing that, after a day or two's march, we found it impossible to go on, we could turn back with less shame and self-reproach than if we had made little or no attempt to carry out our undertaking.

Dr. Todd, who was somewhat of an autocrat on board his ship, waxed angry and contemptuous. Who were these nurses who dared to dispute his opinion? He said that what we did or did not do was a matter of supreme indifference to him. He had offered us the only possible advice — we would not take it—well, our foolhardiness would meet with its just reward. Thereupon he hurled himself out of our tent. The Consul followed meekly, saying he was very sorry, shaking hands, and assuring us that "Todd meant well!"

This episode settled the question of our stay at 'Mpanda's much more expeditiously than would otherwise have been the case, and the very next day we set off with Dr. Glanville to Nevez Fereira, a Portuguese camp about six miles distant. A trader, called Madeira, who lived there was said to have great influence with the natives. He would perhaps procure bearers for us. But, unfortunately; although Madeira was extremely civil, and gave us a capital luncheon; he declared that he could no longer obtain natives even for himself.

Lieutenant Pedro Alvarez, acting Commandante at 'Mpanda's, joined us at luncheon. Like all the Portuguese we met in Africa, he had been most kind to us. Ever since our arrival at 'Mpanda's he had kept us supplied with bread, game, and any other luxury which found its way to his camp. We met a Portuguese army-doctor, too, and after luncheon he took us to see his hospital. Here the sick were established in a hospital tent of the most approved fashion, ventilated on the best principles, cool even on that burning day. It was beautifully kept, too, and was altogether a great contrast to the wretched grass hut which served as a hospital at 'Mpanda's.

Though our tramp to Nevez Fereira was a failure, as far as obtaining bearers was concerned, we were not cast down; and on the way back it was decided that the next day Wilkins should start off to a kraal about fifty miles distant, and do his utmost to secure carriers. He set out early the next morning with a well-known explorer called Moodie, to whom all parts of Africa seemed equally familiar. The same day Mr. Walter Sutton joined our party, the men he had come up with proving most unsatisfactory. Late that same evening the launch of the

Pigeon arrived to take Mr. Jerram and Dr. Todd back to Beira the following day.

We said good-bye to the Vice-Consul with great regret. The Portuguese Commandante was much disgusted at his having to leave. "Who," he exclaimed, "am I to treat with now? there are only traders here—with such people I do not speak!" Fortunately the "people" in question did not hear this speech, or there would have been trouble. As it was, some foolish young fellows nearly created a new Portuguese question, by hoisting a red pocket handkerchief, with a white elephant printed in the centre, on the flagstaff from which the Consul used to fly his Union Jack. The Commandante took the foolish joke to mean an insult to his flag, and it was all Dr. Glanville could do to pacify him.

The camp now became very untidy and rowdy; and as Lieutenant Pedro Alvarez constantly urged our departure, we engaged any likely boy we came across, and resolved that we would start for the interior with only ten boys, without waiting for the return of Wilkins.

At this juncture Mr. Harrison, a well-known prospector, arrived in the camp from Fort Salisbury. Hearing of our difficulty, he gave us his own three boys, making his way to Beira as best he could without them. Those who know anything of African travel will agree that a more unselfish act was never done. He also took the trouble to write out a small vocabulary of the most useful words and phrases in Mashona, and drew out a map of the country—marking the best halting-places, the distances from water to water, and the time we ought to take in getting from place to place. Had his presence at the coast been less urgently needed, he would have turned back and escorted us to Umtali. Mr. Harrison was emphatically a friend in need.

Having now nine boys, we resolved to start on Tuesday, the 30th of June. We spent the morning of the 29th in packing, dividing the provisions into loads of forty pounds each, having been told that this was the correct weight. Then tired, hungry, but hopeful, we sat down to luncheon.

Suddenly a crowd of natives presented themselves at the entrance of our tent. As we gazed at them in wonder, their ranks opened, and there, in the centre, stood Wilkins, leaning on his gun and enjoying our surprise. The hero of melodrama does not achieve a more effective entrance! For quite five minutes Wilkins refused to do more than wave his hand towards his followers, and repeat in a sepulchral voice, "I'm here." At last we persuaded him to come in and have some luncheon, leaving the natives to squat outside.

Gradually Dr. Glanville broke to him the fact that he proposed leaving the next day, but that he expected Wilkins to remain behind in charge of the stores.

I think the poor old man nearly went out of his mind with mortified vanity. He wandered about unpacking everything, taking out food-stuffs, and filling up the loads with saucepan lids. Sister Lucy and I consulted together, and came to the conclusion that the best thing to do was to leave him quite alone; and, in fact, after a great deal of noise and confusion, he retired to his tent and went to sleep.

Just then a man-of-war's launch puffed up to the landing-place, bringing the new Vice-Consul, Lieutenant Robertson of the *Brisk*, who presently came to our tent, and offered us a large supply of oranges for the road. He was very cheery about our enterprise, declaring that though difficult, and even hazardous, it was feasible, and he felt sure we should carry it through successfully. These were the first hopeful words we had heard on the subject, and they did us a world of good.

By the following day the wrath of Wilkins had subsided, but now a fresh difficulty arose. Dr. Doyle Glanville asked, who had money? "This," he said, throwing two sovereigns on the table, "is all the money I possess." We nurses had about £14 between us.

There were between thirty-five and forty carriers; nearly £40 had to be divided between them before they would stir. Neither the Doctor nor Wilkins had any authority from the Bishop to borrow money, and no one in camp would lend it on their word. Wilkins had given most of his ready money to Dr. Knight Bruce, and could only spare a small sum. The situation was very uncomfortable; but in our emergency Lieutenant Robertson came to our aid, lent Dr. Glanville £20, and enabled us to depart.

CHAPTER IV

The start—A "dug-out"—Missing load—A kraal—Native funeral—On the road—Another kraal—Lions—A Portuguese breakfast—No water—Captain Winslow—We meet two white men—Honey-birds—Lions again—Sarmento—A native hunt—Trouble with carriers—Forced march—Masse-Kesse—We lose our way—Illness of Sister Aimée—At last Umtali—The Bishop.

WE left 'Mpanda's about three o'clock in the afternoon, intending to stay a few miles out of the camp, so as to start on our walk early the next morning, the 1st of July. Our departure had been delayed in many ways. The carriers became troublesome; some rushed off to the canteen to drink, others refused to take up their loads. At last we three, with Dr. Glanville and seven boys, started off, accompanied for the first mile or two by the Consul, Mr. Robertson, the Portuguese Commandante, and one or two other men. Mr. Sutton remained behind to drive on the other boys. After about an hour's walking we said farewell to our friends, and pushed on alone,—not for long, however, as the Consul came running after us to say we were on the wrong path. We had to retrace our steps for a long way.

By this time the sun was getting low in the heavens. In Africa when the sun sets, it gets dark almost immediately, there being hardly any twilight. We were therefore very glad to find ourselves once more on the right path, and, soon after, we met Mr. Sutton, who had turned back to look for us. He told us we should have to cross the Pûngwé, to get to the kraal where we meant to make our first encampment. It was almost dark when we reached the river, where we found our carriers and their loads waiting their turn to cross. This took a long time, there being only one little canoe, or "dug-out," paddled by a curious shrivelled-up old native. The "dug-out" is made from the trunk of a tree with the inside scooped out. We three got into it, sitting very carefully on the edges, there being no seats, or even sticks laid across, and it was too narrow to admit of our sitting at the bottom. We were in mortal terror, and almost afraid to breathe, for the least movement upsets these frail little barks, and the river, as we knew, swarmed with crocodiles. It was a great relief to be on *terra firma* again, and to watch the rest of our party crossing.

Night had quite set in by this time; and the shadowy line of carriers, standing at the water's edge, looked strange and unreal. On a high bank above the river we found a small kraal, where we began to make preparations for the night.

A kraal is a native village, composed of either many or few huts, in shape like beehives, into which you literally crawl on hands and knees. The huts are made with a framework of wood, the roof covered with grass, and the sides plastered with mud. The floor also is mud, but beaten into a smooth, hard surface. The ground outside the huts is also beaten into this same hard surface.

Supper was the first thing to prepare, but could not be achieved without lights. We hunted through all our bundles, but could discover no candles or lanterns. To our dismay we found the boy who had charge of this load to be missing. There was nothing to be done, then, but make the best of it. Our boys lighted a fire of mealie stalks and dried reeds, there being no wood anywhere near. It was not a very good fire, for reeds only flare up for a short time, smoulder away, and give no heat. We ate a hasty supper of corned beef and biscuits with a little coffee; rolled ourselves in our blankets, with a waterproof sheet spread over us; and tried to sleep by the fire. To keep it going we had to sacrifice a wooden box, and the two men undertook to replenish it, but Dr. Glanville fell asleep at his post. If it had not been for Sister Aimée, who acted as stoker, we should have come off very badly. All night long we heard the roar of lions in the distance, and every now and then the weird cry of the hyænas, which prowled and rustled in the mealie field. Towards morning we were roused from troubled sleep by frightful yells and lamentations, a sort of dismal chant broken by long sobbing wails. It was really a blood-curdling sound, and for some moments we were afraid to move or speak. At last, seeing that our natives were paying little or no attention to it, we made inquiries, and found that one of the inhabitants of the kraal had just died, and that his people were keening over him, much as mourners do in Ireland. As we got up we were requested to retire to a distant corner of the kraal, and not to cross the path along which the body was to be carried. It was borne away in a very ingenious sort of wicker-work coffin, made of reeds and rushes.

After some little trouble we secured a pail of water, retired into the mealies, and made a rapid toilet, whilst the men boiled some cocoa. When we had partaken of this we could do nothing but wait patiently till our missing boy and his load had been found —we had been obliged to send a runner back to 'Mpanda's to hunt him up. Our difficulties were a good deal increased by the fact that neither Dr. Glanville nor Mr. Sutton could speak a word of the language. We three knew only just enough to ask for water, or a fire, or one or two other things. Again it was Sister Aimée who saved the situation by being able to talk Portuguese. We found to our joy that three or four of our carriers were Portuguese speaking natives, so these boys acted as interpreters between us and the other natives.

It was quite ten o'clock before we could make a real start; however, once off, we did a good day's march over rough, uninteresting ground. We halted for a few minutes every hour or so, walking on these Kaffir paths being very tiring. They are so narrow, and the grass on either side so tall, that there might easily be a number of people a few yards in front of you, and yet you might walk for hours quite unaware of their proximity.

At the first large kraal that we came to, all the village turned out to look at us, we being the first white women they had seen. They presented us with a large jar of "chuali," or native beer, which our carriers drank, and in return we gave them some beads. It is not considered etiquette to pass through any of these native villages without giving the chief a present of some kind— a few "beads" or a stretch of "limbo" will do. A stretch is measured by holding out both arms as far as you can, and measuring from finger-tip to finger-tip. Roughly speaking, one gives about two yards. With this we could buy a good deal of meal from natives, who preferred it to money.

Soon after we left this kraal we found the path very rough, and the walking difficult; the heat also became intense; and, being unused to marching, we began to get very weary. At about three o'clock we came to another large village, and found, to our regret, that the natives would go no farther, and that we should have to spend the night there. These kraals are very dirty and noisy. After a delightful bath in the Pûngwé, during which we kept in shallow water looking out for crocodiles, we felt much revived, and set to work and cooked quite a splendid dinner of eggs and fowl procured from the natives. Our boys made a sort of "lean-to" with a few poles, grass, and their loads. We had a fairly good night, but found the ground very hard; and the lions were so near, that we could hear the pig-like grunt they make when they are hunting. By this time we were so accustomed to them that we were much less terrified of them, and almost began to look upon them as bores that kept one awake when one was sleepy.

The next morning we got off fairly early. The men were very lazy, and we had to rouse them always, get breakfast ready, and start the camp. Our path led us across the Pûngwé again, but this time we were each carried over on the shoulders of two boys, the ford not being deep. The other boys plunged in, making a great noise, shouting, and beating the water, to frighten away the crocodiles. A Portuguese hut was built on the opposite bank, and here an agent of the Mozambique Company lived. Like all Portuguese he was extremely kind and courteous, and gave us an excellent breakfast. After leaving the hut we had a long march of about fifteen miles without water. The track crossed a burnt-up plain, and then lost itself in a long stretch of loose sand, where at every step forward one seemed to slip two back. Trying as it is to walk through grass that is ten feet high, coarse, strong, slashing your face as you push your way through, we were glad when we came to patches of it, because of the slender shade it afforded. Like all novices at such work, we had, early in the day, impatiently drained the water bottles. Then came some hours during which we suffered considerably from thirst before we reached any water. This we did late in the afternoon, when we came upon some rude bamboo huts beside a dismal swamp. Captain Winslow, of H.M.S. *Brisk*, whom we met shortly after leaving the Portuguese hut, had slept there the night before, and had had one of the huts cleaned out, so that, after the floor was covered with a pile of fresh grass, we found it very comfortable. In the other shelter a young Englishman was dining. We confiscated his coffee, drinking it up in the twinkling of an eye. No coffee has ever tasted or ever could taste like that. We longed for water, but dared not touch it till it had been boiled. Even when made into tea it tasted of swamp. This young Englishman, whose coffee we absorbed, was on his way up country. He seemed to have suffered a good deal from fever, and was even then light-headed. The friend who was travelling with him had followed a honey-bird, and soon came back to the hut with the honey in a sort of palm-leaf basket. The honey-bird is a curious little creature, something like a water-wagtail. It comes fluttering about a man till he follows it, and then it leads him to some hollow tree, or cleft in a rock, which is full of honey. It seems to know that, without the help of man, it cannot obtain the spoil it covets. When the combs are rifled, one is always left for the little feathered guide; otherwise, the natives say, it will never again lead anyone to a bees' nest. We saw numbers of these honey-birds, but of course could not follow them.

The night spent in this shelter might have been passed outside a lion's cage in the Zoo. The lions, coming down to drink at the swampy pool just in front of our huts, made such a terrific noise that the earth seemed to shake with their roaring. It was a strange sensation to find ourselves so near all these wild creatures, with not even the slenderest door or mat to shut them out of our hut. In the morning the spoor of an elephant was seen, which the young fellow who had followed the honey-bird spoored, and shot a few hours later. His name was Carrick, one of our model patients later on at Umtali, and still a valued friend.

The next morning we were up at the dawn of day, reaching Sarmento early in the afternoon. Our path lay through a beautiful park-like country, with big trees dotted about, and here and there great clumps of palm-trees. We passed many herd of game, great buffaloes quietly grazing, who stood and looked at us, but hardly took the trouble to move out of our way, and troops of every kind of deer—wildebeest, hartebeest, water-buck, etc. The men who were with us evidently knew little about shooting. Several futile attempts were made to get a buck, but the guns either went off unexpectedly, or else refused to go off at all. The natives, who are very keen sportsmen, lost all patience, threw down their bundles, and proceeded to hunt a buffalo on their own account, and succeeded in killing him with their assegais after some little time. Then, covered with blood, they trotted after us to Sarmento, with great lumps of gory flesh tied on to their bundles. The Bishop's bag, containing his robes, was not spared, and his spotless lawn was deeply stained.

Sarmento is nearly forty-five miles from 'Mpanda's; we reached it in about two days and a half. It was not such bad walking as English people might think. Time must be allowed for fording streams, and getting through swamps and long grass; and the great heat must also be taken into account. Like most Portuguese villages, Sarmento was very dirty, but it is a lovely spot, situated on a high plateau, embedded in trees, with the broad Pûngwé rushing below, dashing over great rocks, with trees drooping over the water. We found the Portuguese extremely civil. Mr. Almaida, the Mozambique Company's agent, kindly placed his own hut at our disposal, sending us wine, eggs, candles, etc., and doing all he could to make us comfortable.

The next day we were off betimes, all much refreshed by the rest. We began now to feel a little uneasy about our carriers, for we knew that their own kraal lay somewhere near at hand. We had been warned that we should experience no little difficulty in getting them past this place. They left Sarmento at a tremendous pace, with a good deal of singing and shouting. About ten o'clock we arrived at a large kraal, and here, to our consternation, the bearers insisted on staying all day. It was their own home, and no inducement could tear them away. The wily "induna," or captain, hid in the woods, and could not be found till nightfall. So we had to spend the interval as best we could, bathing in the river, and wandering in the wood.

All the men and women in this village came and scraped their feet against the ground in front of us — a native mode of salutation — and we gave the usual present of beads or limbo. Then there came some very old women with baskets of lovely white meal, which they laid at Sister Aimée's feet. This, I believe, is considered rather an unusual honour, for as a rule the natives are very chary of giving away meal, which constitutes their principal food. Towards dusk the chief reappeared and demanded blankets for all his boys. Dr. Glanville became very angry and drove him off. In consequence of this we had a sleepless night. For the Doctor and Mr. Sutton — being afraid the boys would not only run away, but might attack us—sat up all night with loaded guns, a demonstration not a little alarming to us, considering that neither of them appeared to know much about firearms. However, nothing happened, but the next morning the induna came with his men, and laid all the money received from us down at Sister Aimée's feet, declaring they would go no farther. After a very long talk they consented to proceed on condition of receiving extra blankets at Masse-Kesse. The fact that none of us could talk to them in their own language left us at a great disadvantage. The whole party depending on Sister Aimée's small knowledge of Portuguese, we could not feel sure that our Portuguese native translated our wishes faithfully. The white men of our party lost much prestige with the carriers through being unable to give them any orders. These wild natives do not understand being commanded by women, who as a rule represent to them nothing but the chief domestic animal, intended only for hewing wood, carrying water, grinding corn, and so on.

Once off, the boys went splendidly through a lovely bit of country, full of tall palms, banana trees, and great groves of feathery bamboos. Pretty as it was we were anxious to get through it as quickly as we could; for a white traveller, who had given us a plan of the country, had written against this place two ominous words, " Ware lions."

The next two days were wet and rather miserable. We got soaked to the skin as we walked through the long, wet grass. The boys too went badly, wanting to stop at every opportunity. We had great difficulty in starting them at all in the mornings. We could not get properly dry at night, for the fires burnt badly on account of the rain. The rude grass shelters that the boys put up for us to sleep in at night were hardly water-tight. Hyænas made night hideous, coming quite close to our little camp. I think the shriek these animals utter is more objectionable than the cry of any other wild beast. It fills one with shuddering horror, and is more like the wail of a lost soul than a mere earthly sound.

We met two white men the next morning returning to 'Mpanda's with a letter from the Bishop, who was terribly in want of stores. This acted as a kind of spur, and we pushed on with renewed energy. Soon the sun came out, and we reached Mandanjiva, a deserted Portuguese village, perfectly dry, and again in good spirits. Here we had a delightful bathe; and tried to settle down for the night in a dirty, huge, barn-like shelter, open on all sides but one. However, the hyænas drove away sleep by their terrible noise, and even went so far as to sniff round our barn. We were not sorry, therefore, when morning dawned, and we could hasten away from this dreary place.

Now the road became dreadful. There were hours of walking through grass ten feet high; through tall rushes that slashed one's face; through small bogs and shallow streams into which we dashed, boots and all, much to the delight of the boys, but to the horror of our white escort. However, the sun dries one almost at once, and it saved endless time. Here and there we met unfortunate young fellows who had had the fever; had tried to reach Fort Salisbury; but, alas! had been obliged to turn back, and were then on their way down to the coast, ill and half ruined. They gave us terrible accounts of the state of things up country, and appeared to look on us as half mad for attempting to go on. We gave them provisions, and sped them on their way.

All went well with us till we reached Chimoio, a large kraal and Portuguese station. Here the Bishop had been nearly shot, being taken for a Portuguese officer. Mr. Fiennes, who was commanding the Chartered Company's Police, happily recognised him in time. The Bishop's arrival prevented a fight between the Portuguese and Company's people. He told them that the convention between England and Portugal had been signed. The kraal of Chimoio was situated in the midst of a lovely country with wooded hills, great rocks and crags all round. The natives here seemed much less friendly, and we had considerable difficulty in buying a fowl from them for supper. We tried to obtain a runner to send on to Umtali, to announce our near approach to the Bishop, who thought of us as still being at 'Mpanda's; but this we were unable to do.

Retiring to rest between ten and eleven, we were roused by our faithful Portuguese speaking boys, with the terrible announcement that all the carriers had fled. Having built us a shelter, these four boys, who proudly called themselves "the household servants," had gone to sleep in a little hut close by. Waking to make up the fire, they had seen the last of our carriers vanishing in the distance. Dr. Glanville and Mr. Sutton immediately started in pursuit, but of course never even caught a glimpse of the fleet natives. There we were stranded with four boys, seventy miles from Umtali, surrounded by our stores and no means of taking them with us! It is bad enough for men to be abandoned on the veldt : for women, of course, it was worse.

At first we felt rather miserable, but lamentations were useless. What was to be done? that was the question. A council was held, and it was decided that Dr. Glanville, ourselves, and three boys, should push on to Umtali, leaving Mr. Sutton with one boy to look after the stores till we could send and rescue him. After this was settled we composed ourselves as best we could for the few remaining hours that were left before daylight. A few necessaries were hastily packed—we left most of our blankets behind us—and with three days' biscuits, beef, and tea, set out for Umtali on the 4th of July. Just as we were leaving the village we came across a camp of white men, who had arrived during the night, and who proceeded to Umtali a few hours after ourselves. They all turned out to stare at us, saying it was wonderful we should have got so far, but shaking their heads at the idea of our reaching Umtali in four days' time. Defying their predictions, we went on, and kept up a really good pace all day, halting for the night in a lovely wood, where we had a delicious bath in an ice-cold mountain stream. We found the ground somewhat hard, having so few blankets, but in spite of this we passed a tolerably good night.

The next morning we made an early start, and after about an hour's walk found ourselves in a terrible swamp. The boys and their loads got through with difficulty, and then came back to carry us over the worst places, into which they sank sometimes above their waists. It was an unpleasant experience, some of these bogs being like quicksands, swallowing unfortunate people alive. We heard afterwards that two boys had been lost there that year. However, we all got through safely, and went on climbing over mountain sides, even wading through deep streams so as not to wear out our three already heavily-laden boys by making them carry us across. At nightfall we found ourselves outside Masse-Kesse. We were told that this walk from Chimoio to Masse-Kesse was then the quickest on record, so we were inclined to give ourselves great airs, as of "African travellers." However, we certainly seemed to have got over the ground more quickly than the average man did in those early days, which was very creditable.

Just before reaching Masse-Kesse we met a Mr. Paterson. He too brought us a note from the Bishop, in which he said how much he should like to see us, but how impossible it seemed to get us up to our destination. Mr. Paterson was much astonished to see us with only three boys, no tents, no machilas—in fact, it was difficult to make him believe that we were alone, and had not a trail of carriers somewhere behind in the bush.

Masse-Kesse was a red earth fort, standing on a small eminence in the midst of lovely surroundings. I believe this fort was well built, and imagined as a defence against natives, but it could be of no use against Europeans. As we saw it, the walls were partly battered down, and over the great entrance there still remained a big V.R., which the English had put up and the Portuguese had not removed. The country round was lovely. On the horizon one saw a semicircle of mountains, the nearer ones wooded to the summit; whilst beyond one caught a glimpse of blue, rocky peaks melting away into the distance. The plain was covered with tall waving grass, and it was only on closer inspection that one saw how rank and coarse it was. At a distance it might fairly well have been taken for corn-fields or hay-meadows before the harvest. I have been told that hundreds of years ago monks lived at Masse-Kesse, who planted orange trees and lemon groves, the fruit of which we still eat in this nineteenth century of ours.

We found the Commandante at Masse-Kesse exceedingly civil; which was more than we had any right to expect, considering how the Portuguese had been treated by the English. He kindly sent one of his own boys over to Umtali, a distance of eighteen miles, to warn the Bishop of our very unexpected arrival. We hoped by this means to save him from inconvenience.

After quitting the fort we lost our way, and had to encamp in a wood early in the afternoon, whilst our boys went to a kraal some miles distant to obtain what information they could about the way to Umtali. The next day we set off early, and hoped to reach our destination after a few hours' walking. We were obliged to make a forced march, because our provisions had run short. There was indeed nothing left but a little tea and half a pot of bovril.

This was the hardest day of all. A bad rocky path; hill after hill to climb; valleys and ravines to cross; burning heat; and, worst of all, for some hours we could find no water. Even the boys, who seem made of iron, began to lag. As to Sister Aimée she looked half dead. I was terribly anxious about her, feeling sure she must have fever, for, as I took her hand, her skin seemed to burn me. When we did finally reach Umtali her temperature was 105°. Those of my readers who have had even a slight touch of fever will know better than I can tell them what she must have suffered, whilst forcing herself along in that condition. At last we came to a small stream, where we bathed our faces, rinsing out our mouths, as we did not dare to drink much in our heated state. Much refreshed, we longed to light a fire and make some bovril, but there was no wood to be found anywhere near, so we had to go on. After another couple of hours' walking, we came to a larger stream in a grove of bananas, and here we halted and made some soup. This reviving us somewhat, we felt able to make a fresh effort. Then there were more hills to climb, more valleys and ravines to cross, interspersed with long stretches of tall grass, which after a time had a most bewilderingly dizzy effect. At last, towards sunset, Dr. Glanville descried a distant flag—Umtali! The sight of that flag gave us new spirit. We now felt sure we were on the right road, which before had seemed very doubtful,—our Portuguese boy never being able to say anything more reassuring than, " It appears that it may be the right road; it appears that it may not be." Half an hour's quick marching brought us to a small river. As Sister Aimée was scrambling over a fallen tree, which served as a bridge, a hand was suddenly stretched out to help her. It was the Bishop! He looked extremely well, and welcomed us warmly. He had only received our note an hour or two before, and was preparing his hut for us. He was horrified to find Sister Aimée so ill; indeed, by this time it was all we could do to get her up the steep hill, on the top of which the Bishop was then staying. To my great joy I found I could give her half a cup of milk, this being the first time for many weeks that we had seen fresh milk. The next few days passed like a horrible nightmare. Fever even when one has every convenience is unpleasant enough. But a bad attack in the wilds of Africa, with nothing to mitigate it, only the hard earth to lie on, and insufficient blankets, is something not easily forgotten. For many days Sister Aimée gave us cause for grave anxiety, but as soon as she had turned the corner she quickly recovered.

CHAPTER V

Sabi Ophir—Illness of Dr. Glanville—Dr. Lichfield—Lieutenant Eustace Fiennes—No boots—High prices—Maquaniqua the queen—Arrival of Mr. Sutton—Holy Communion—Captain Heany—Sad death of Dr. Glanville—Site of the Mission farm—Appearance of Colonel Pennefather.

THE huts in which we were now established belonged to a Mr. Campion, the manager of the Sabi Ophir Mining Company. They were square and small. We three nurses occupied one, which had been rudely divided into two; Mr. Campion a still smaller one; the Bishop a third. Dr. Glanville was accommodated in a tent. The encampment was perched on the top of a steep, rocky hill, and in the space in front of the huts an enormous tree of the fig species spread forth its branches. This was the only large tree in the whole district, and Sabi Ophir Hill was known to the natives as the "hill of the great tree."

As soon as Sister Aimée was sufficiently recovered to admit of any work being done in the hut, our host set his boys to work, and caused rude stretchers to be put up for us. These were composed of a rough framework, attached to poles driven into the earth, along which branches were tied, so as to form a rough kind of lattice work. Over this a few bundles of grass were laid, and, lo! you had a bed! It was much pleasanter to sleep on one of these stretchers than on the floor, as one could escape from the ants, and in some degree from the rats. It was not, however, the perfection of comfort, as one woke up every morning bruised and aching, and covered from head to foot with a neat impression of the lattice work on which one had lain. The Bishop had his air-bed with him, and kindly lent it to Sister Aimée for the days when she was at the worst, and she found it a great comfort.

The forced march from Chimoio to Umtali had told on Dr. Glanville, so Dr. Knight Bruce gave him two days' rest before sending him back with carriers to relieve Mr. Sutton. He started on the return journey on Friday, the 17th of July, but, to our surprise and dismay, he returned unexpectedly on the following Monday, in a strangely exhausted condition, and unable to give any account of himself. One native was with him, and explained that "the white man" had fallen ill, had halted at a kraal, had sent the carriers on to Chimoio's, and had remained lying down and "talking foolish" till that morning. The Doctor was still inclined to "talk foolish," and was in a very strange condition both physically and mentally.

The Bishop sent over to the Police camp for Dr. Lichfield, who arrived shortly after. He pronounced Dr. Glanville to be "very tired," which was obvious, and ordered feeding up and rest. To rest was easy, to be fed up difficult. We had nothing but the Chartered Company's musty meal and fly-stricken ox. The latter luxury often failed us, nor was it, at its best, tempting. Again Mr. Campion came to the rescue with fowls and a few eggs, so that in a day or so our patient was sufficiently improved to discuss future plans with the Bishop.

The result of the discussion was that Dr. Glanville severed his connection with the Mission, and, having some acquaintances in the Police camp, appealed to them for the means of going on to Salisbury.

Foremost amongst these friends was Lieutenant Eustace Fiennes, brother of the present Lord Saye and Sele, whom we came to regard as a sort of special providence. He saved us as far as possible from the inevitable difficulties that beset inexperienced pioneers like ourselves, and was invariably kind, courteous, and helpful—to say nothing of being a very jolly young fellow and excellent company. Nothing, indeed, could have exceeded the kindness of both officers and men of the Chartered Company's Police. We take this opportunity of thanking them individually and collectively for all they did for us.

Meanwhile we heard nothing about the hospital, and, after waiting a little for the Bishop to speak, we at last asked him what had been settled. He said that he had been to Salisbury, and, having seen the Administrator, had decided not to open a Mission hospital, but to establish us in one which the Company would build. He had, accompanied by Mr. Duncan, the Surveyor-General, chosen a spot near the site of his own Mission farm, and here the Chartered Company would put up wattle and daub buildings as soon as possible.

For the moment we could not go and see this site; for, having been unable to bring much luggage from Chimoio, and hoping that Mr. Sutton would be able to engage boys and follow us immediately, we had merely taken food and blankets with us. We were in consequence shoeless, the last three days of rough and rapid marching having almost torn our boots off our feet, though they had been in excellent condition as far as Chimoio. What I called "boots" consisted of a collection of rags bound to my feet with bandages. Sisters Lucy Sleeman and B. Welby were in much the same condition. We could not explore the country, or do more than potter about in front of our huts.

Just before our arrival a trader had made his way to Umtali from Fort Salisbury. He brought some provisions, but no candles. At that time of year the sun sets at about six o'clock, darkness descends on the earth immediately, and it does not become light again till nearly seven in the morning. The long hours of darkness, during which we lived in an enforced state of idleness, were very trying. In the Police camp "one farthing dip" was sold for a guinea. Sometimes this treasure was raffled for—the fortunate seller exacting money down, and the right to sit with the candle. Mr. Fiennes contrived to send us two or three, which were made to last for weeks.

One morning a Mashona queen, aunt of M'Tassa, the kinglet of Manica, came to see us. She was a powerful chieftainess, owning sway over many kraals in the valley watered by the Revue river, and stretching away from Umtali towards Masse-Kesse. At the battle of Chua, before referred to, she brought her natives to fight for the Chartered Company, and led them herself; and when they ran away, as Mashonas generally do, smashed in with her battle-axe the heads of as many runaways as she could catch. She herself remained under fire with the utmost composure. Her name was Maquaniqua. The "Queen" stalked up to the great fig-tree before our door, and squatted under it, sending a man, bearing her curious battle-axe of black wood elaborately inlaid with brass, to announce her arrival to us. Another native brought presents to us. These were somewhat unworthy of a great potentate, consisting as they did of a basket of meal, two eggs, and six sweet potatoes. It was clearly a case of accepting the will for the deed!

Maquaniqua was a fine specimen of animal humanity, with a splendid coarse physique, and an ugly, brutal face. She accepted tea, passing her mug, after drinking, to the two men who sat behind her. These were two of her husbands. We were told that she had several, whom she divorced or knocked on the head as seemed most convenient. Curiously enough, in the kraals governed by a chieftainess the other women are in a state of, if possible, more abject subjection than when under the rule of a chief. The men seem to revenge on their wives the respect they are forced to show to their queen.

Maquaniqua, at first interesting and amusing, soon became an awful bore. We could not get rid of her. When the tea, jam, and cookies were finished, when she had delivered a message from M'Tassa to the effect that the "white women" were welcome, though he was too great a personage to pay them a visit, we hoped she would go. Not at all! She demanded "fire-water," and was much disappointed at not receiving any. Then she took a fancy to a bright tin plate—all our plates were tin, bright, new, and glittering, therefore like silver. Should we sacrifice a precious plate, and so deliver ourselves from this swarthy incubus? We consulted together, and finally decided on presenting the plate, with an intimation that, after so splendid a present, the white women would not consider her polite if she remained. One of the Mission natives who could speak English interpreted. Our intimation had the desired effect. A German master of the ceremonies is not a greater stickler for etiquette than an African chief or chieftainess. As Maquaniqua got up to leave, her escort, clapping their hands in token of respect, trotted away; the chieftainess striding after them, having first handed her plate to one of her husbands to carry, and giving the other a little packet of brown sugar which she had obtained from us.

That same day Mr. Sutton arrived from Chimoio, greatly to our delight. The poor lad had been very ill indeed with fever, and while he was lying in a state of extreme exhaustion some white men came into the wretched shelter in which he lay, pronounced him to be "doosid dicky," and not likely to "pull out," and forthwith—after helping themselves to food, his knife, his kettle, and any other appliance they required—left him to his fate. Fortunately the carriers from Umtali arrived the next day, and in a short time he was on his legs again. He very pluckily set out for Umtali, almost as soon as he could stand. It is astonishing how quickly that African fever prostrates a man, and with what equal rapidity he recovers—or dies—as the case may be. This is perhaps true only of its first attacks. Later on, when a man is saturated with malaria, he seems unable to shake off the fever. The recurrences are slight, but persistent, and it is then that complications arise and health is completely undermined.

The day after Mr. Sutton's arrival was Sunday, and the Bishop held a celebration. We were at our wit's end to arrange for this ceremony, which was to take place in the hut where the Bishop slept, and where there was a rough table made of reeds and boughs of trees. With a little white limbo we contrived to make this look presentable, but there was neither chalice nor patten. What were we to do? We had one or two battered enamelled tin mugs to drink out of, supplementing deficient tea-cups with empty cocoa-tins. These, of course, were not to be thought of. On our consulting the Bishop, he suggested that a metal cup belonging to a flask in which brown sugar used to appear might do. Nothing else being available we turned out the sugar, polished the cup to the utmost, and reluctantly placed it on the improvised communion table. To such straits is a missionary bishop sometimes reduced!

On Monday Dr. Knight Bruce left Sabi Ophir to go and live at the spot selected for his farm, where he had had some huts put up. Mr. Sutton accompanied him, volunteering his services till such time as the Mission could fill the vacancy left by Dr. Glanville. This gentleman had found a friend in need in the person of Captain Heany of the Road-Making Company, better known as the leader of the Mashonaland Pioneers, whose entry into the hitherto unexplored country had paved the way for the British South Africa Company's Police.

This pioneer captain was ever ready to stretch a helping hand to those in need. Indeed, his reckless generosity finally somewhat crippled his resources, which, though large, were not unlimited. He hailed from Virginia, owned kinship with Edgar Allan Poe, and, under the somewhat rough exterior of a pioneer, concealed refined tastes and unexpected culture. He was, deservedly, one of the most popular men in Mashonaland. To him everyone went for help or advice; and, wherever he built his hut, a rude village was certain to spring up in a few days. Captain Heany, then, supplied Dr. Glanville with food, money, and boys; and also procured for him the charge of Sir John Willoughby's horses, which had to be sent to Salisbury. By this means it was hoped that the Doctor would reach his destination safely, without undue fatigue.

He came to bid us farewell before leaving, and seemed in better health and spirits than he had been since we left 'Mpanda's. We were never destined to meet again, for the poor fellow died by the roadside within a few miles of Salisbury. No white man was with him during his last moments, nor is anything known of them. Of his three boys, two remained with him. The third went on to Salisbury; reported his death; and guided Dr. Rand, of the Company's Police, and Mr. Hay to the spot. They found that Dr. Glanville must have been dead for more than a day. He lay rolled in his blankets, the boys squatting by a fire at a little distance. The horses were tied up close at hand. There was no food in the bundles, though he had left Umtali well supplied. They buried him where he lay, a blazed tree marking his last resting-place. The news of his death did not reach Umtali for a considerable time. Those were not the days of rapid communication.

To return to Manica. One of our first expeditions was to see the projected site of the hospital—a distance of about two miles from Sabi Ophir across the veldt.

Descending from our eyrie, and crossing by a slippery pole a rapid torrent which rushed at the foot of the hill, we wound along, passing beneath the height on which the Police camp was pitched. The Bishop was with us, and he was amused to see all the natives who were working in the camp tear madly down the slope with a view of catching a glimpse of the "m'lungas," or white women. Their masters rushed out too, ostensibly to recall their boys, but possibly with a desire to see what the new importations were like. I think at that time there were over two hundred police in Manica, and we had only made acquaintance with a few of them.

Leaving the camp behind we hastened on after our guide; crossed one or two streams on stepping-stones; climbed a height or two, and at last found ourselves on the summit of a grassy slope, backed by towering rocks and thick bush, where our huts were to be built. Already poles and grass for one hut were cut and ready for use.

The hill on which we stood commanded a splendid view of the grassy plains of the long narrow valley, rolling away in park-like stretches, and broken here and there by a clump of trees, or a pile of gigantic granite boulders called "kopjes." Though we could not catch the glint of water, a long line of thick, dwarf bush, winding like a serpent along the valley, betrayed the course of the river. Hills, piled up tier upon tier—some thickly wooded, some bare and rocky—shut in the horizon. Truly Manica is a fair land and a goodly heritage, which he who once held would be very loth to let go, and is well worth a fight. African travellers declare it to be one of the most beautiful spots on the Dark Continent. A sort of tropical Switzerland, its rich gold-fields are perhaps the least of its attractions. But the dragon which must be overcome, before its wealth and beauty can be enjoyed, is the fever, which civilisation will soon make short work of. When the railway unites Manicaland to the coast, good food and sufficient clothing will be within reach of every one; huts will give place to water-tight houses; and the long, rank grass will vanish before the increasing population. In those days very little will be heard of malarial fever, and the Utopian dreams of farmer and miner will probably be more than realised. It is impossible to travel through these immense fertile solitudes, without a feeling of intense wonder and regret that so many thousands of human beings should live, their whole lives herded together in the pestilential slums of European cities. Karma — undoubtedly a clear case of Karma!

The quasi-civilisation of Johannesburg and Kimberley had not initiated us into the difficulties of pioneer life, though our experiences in those places were useful in many ways. We were delighted with the place of our future abode, and looked forward, without *arrière pensée*, to opening a hospital there.

It was Mr. Fiennes who first raised a note of alarm. He told us that the innocent-looking brook we had slipped over so easily became a raging river during the rains. It would cut off the hospital from all communication with the Police camp for days together. The only doctor in the place lived in the camp, it must be remembered, and all our provisions came from there. Mr. Fiennes added that the "doctor's assistant," of whom we had heard, existed only on paper. It would be quite impossible, he said, for three women to live alone on that hill, two miles from the doctor or from any help whatsoever. If a patient were taken worse at night, we could send no message to Dr. Lichfield till morning. Not a native would ever be induced to cross the veldt at night; nor would it be fair to ask it in a country where wild beasts were plentiful. In the interests of future patients we must make a stand, and refuse to have our hospital on the site chosen for it.

Here was indeed a dilemma! We clearly saw the force of Mr. Fiennes's reasons, but we did not see how to get matters remedied. We laid the case before the Bishop, but he explained that he could not interfere in the matter. It was, he said, entirely a question for the Company to decide. Still he would not disapprove of our efforts to obtain more suitable arrangements. He would even help us indirectly. Then began a sort of game of battledore and shuttlecock. A. referred us and our protestations to B., B. to C., C. sent us back to A., and nothing was done. At last our excellent host, Mr. Campion, suggested an appeal to Captain Heany.

Eagerly catching at any advice which seemed reasonable, and knowing Captain Heany's influence to be very great, we set off to his camp that very afternoon, and asked his counsel and help. Both were given very readily, and at a word from him quite a commotion was created in the country. The diggers and traders unanimously agreed that they would have nothing to do with the proposed hospital if it were placed on that spot, and would if necessary build one for themselves. A subscription list was opened, and a considerable sum was sent to us the next day.

Just at that time Colonel Pennefather, of the Inniskillings, who was commanding the Chartered Company's Police, came from Salisbury to Umtali, and made a pilgrimage to our camp on Sabi Ophir Hill. We found him delightful to deal with. With the prompt decision of a soldier he had the vexed question settled in a day, and it was resolved that we should occupy a small encampment close to the Police lines. Hospital huts would be built near it, and in two or three weeks we should be able to receive patients.

CHAPTER VI

Settling down at Sabi Ophir—Difficulties of cooking—No luggage — Gold panning — Mr. Sutton leaves the Bishop—Description of our huts—Visit from a hyæna—Arrival of Mrs. Tulloch and children—The question of food—Flowers—Mr. Selous visits Umtali—Mr. Teal devoured by a lion—The native labour question—Evils of drink—Our boxes are rifled by the natives—Our first patient — The Administrator arrives at Umtali — Hospital hut opened — Bishop leaves for England — Horrors of night duty — Arrival of Mr. Rhodes—Site of camp moved—The rains begin—Mr. and Mrs. Bent.

AFTER this excitement life settled back into monotonous idleness. We endeavoured to make our leisure useful by acquiring a knowledge of cookery, but truly it was learning pursued under difficulties. We had rations of coarse meal and a piece of ox flesh. Our cooking utensils consisted of a three-legged pot and a frying-pan.

How were we to create a dinner? A year later we should have produced something eatable; but in those days we were incapable. We boiled the ox flesh in the three-legged pot, whence it issued in the condition of shoe-leather. Mixing the meal with water, we made the most horrible half-cooked flat cakes by heating the dough on hot stones. There was neither baking powder nor yeast in the country.

One day we received a present of venison, shot by a Mr. Teal. Now, I had from time to time saved up a small quantity of sardine oil, believing myself to be a famous housekeeper. In a moment of vain self-confidence I undertook the dinner that night, and we invited Mr. Campion to come and eat venison steaks. I fried these steaks in my sardine oil, and served them proudly. They positively looked like real steaks, such as people would eat at home. But, alas! scarcely had two mouthfuls been eaten when every one fled from the table, and my wonderful dinner was abandoned to the little native who waited on us. He certainly enjoyed it immensely, so even that ill wind blew somebody good; but it was unanimously decided that henceforth I was never to be trusted with the preparation of meals, and I was reduced to the position of a kitchen-maid—not, I must confess, before it was high time.

Rumours now reached us that the Road Company's waggons had at last arrived at 'Mpanda's, and had begun their return trek. Then we heard of oxen dying, of long delays on the road, and of fever amongst the trekkers, some of whom were said to have died. Captain Heany sent fresh teams of oxen and waggons down to bring up the travellers, giving orders that our luggage was to be secured and brought up. The Mission people abandoned the waggons, and trailed up to Umtali, one after the other, each bringing a few boys and some provisions. One of them reached Umtali on the 10th of August, and told us that old Wilkins was stuck at Chimoio with all the luggage. The oxen were dead, and he could do nothing till the fresh teams arrived. It was quite impossible to say when we should get our clothes; meanwhile we should have to go on with the couple of changes of linen we had had with us on the march, and be very thankful if we ever again beheld our boxes. We had made a resolution never to grumble, and on the whole I think we kept it fairly well.

Meanwhile digging and prospecting went on actively; gold reefs were discovered in every direction; no one talked of anything but "booms," "shares," "quartz carrying visible," and the prospect of finding alluvial fields. It was amusing to go to a digger's encampment, see him "crush" his quartz, and then "pan it." Panning means washing the crushed quartz in a sort of iron basin, gradually allowing all the rubbish to flow away with the water, and then the heavy gold remains in the bottom of a pan in a thin yellow streak, often almost imperceptible. When a miner sees this yellow streak he exclaims that he has "got colour," and is a happy man. Finding a great deal of colour is a reason for "going on the burst." Finding nothing at all is also a reason for a "burst." Thus do extremes meet.

Old Wilkins reached Umtali on the 16th of August, having left the luggage at Chimoio to come up with Captain Heany's waggons. Shortly after Mr. Sutton left the Mission, returning to Sabi Ophir. He was such a good-natured young fellow that we felt sure the Bishop would miss him. He said he did not find that the life at the Mission agreed with him, and preferred seeking for work elsewhere. Very soon after his arrival at Sabi Ophir we left that encampment, and took possession of four huts about fifty yards from the lines. The officers furnished these huts for us, and made them astonishingly comfortable. They stripped their own huts of the spoils of Masse-Kesse, and we became the proud possessors of a real table, chairs, a pair of candlesticks, and treasure of treasures! —a bath. The huts were of a round beehive shape; the mud walls were concealed behind a drapery of blue and white limbo, and the earthen floors covered with the white mats which the natives weave out of split reeds. These mats are extremely practical, as they are strong and capable of being washed.

Our encampment was enclosed by a low wall of loosely piled stones, inside which we were assured no wild beast would dare to penetrate. We firmly believed this, and felt quite safe till an enterprising hyæna tried to enter into our store hut, where a piece of ox was suspended from the roof awaiting to be consumed. I consider it a special providence that no wild creatures burst into our sleeping huts. We had no doors, only a mat hanging before the opening. Many a night did we lie awake in terror, listening to the strange, uncanny noises of the veldt, and imagining every sort of terrible possibility. We tried to overcome these terrors, with but indifferent success; and I cannot say that we ever became accustomed to the neighbourhood of wild beasts.

About this time a prospector, named Tulloch, brought his wife and two little children from the coast in machilas. We went to see Mrs. Tulloch, and found her in bed with a slight attack of fever; the two children were ill also. It was strange and delightful to see children again. We made Mrs. Tulloch promise to bring them over to see us as soon as possible. Like ourselves, this family had been forced to leave all their luggage behind them, and were in want of provisions. It was a great regret to us that we could not help them. We had nothing ourselves but the Company's rations, on which even the men could not, and were not expected, to live.

The kindness of the Company's officers kept us from starvation. The meat rations often failed to appear, or were uneatable. Such incidents must be expected in a new country, but it was very unpleasant to be conscious that, instead of being able to help, we were ourselves a burden on the already heavily taxed resources of the camp. But there was nothing to be done but accept the situation till Dr. Jameson, the Administrator, came down from Salisbury. Meanwhile every prospector who came to see us brought an offering. One came with a bake-pot, one with bananas, one with honey in a bottle. Mr. Fiennes, who had some cows, sent milk regularly to us and to Mrs. Tulloch. A Mashona cow that gives three wine bottles of milk a day is considered a good cow, so that the bottle of milk which we received every day was a very generous gift, and proved a great boon as soon as we had any bad case to nurse.

I may seem to lay great stress on our feeding experiences, but in Africa the food question is really a burning one. How to obtain provisions, how to cook them when procured—these are problems of absorbing interest in a pioneer camp.

It is curious and interesting to watch the process of victualling a new country, which is cut off from ordinary transport organisation. The first thing a trader asks himself is, "What will sell best?" The answer is not far to seek—whisky! Thereupon he buys up the cheapest spirit he can obtain in the colony, engages seventy or eighty natives to "run it up," and floods the country with fiery poison. To make up the carrier's loads to the requisite weight he adds a few conveniently-sized tins of food stuff. He does not care in the least what sort of food it is, relying as he does for all his profit on the whisky. Spirit which he has bought for 15s. the dozen, he sells for 30s. a bottle, and considers that he is barely making a fair profit. Meanwhile the provisions he throws on the market are most eccentric. I remember a time when nothing but sardines could be bought in Umtali. Then came a period of tinned lobster, to be followed by a deluge of foie-gras. For a week or two the whole of Manica breakfasted, dined, supped on foie-gras—not of the best. A great deal of illness which was attributed to fever and climate might with much truth be put down to the score of eccentric eating and drinking.

Among the things which disappointed us in Africa were the flowers. There were a good many, it is true, and very brilliant ones, but they came out in successions, like crops, and so the varied effect so beautiful in England was entirely lost. Whilst the hospital huts were in process of construction we used to go on flower-hunting expeditions, knowing that soon we should have no time for wanderings. With the exception of a tall flag-like lily, which grew along the banks of rivers, or in pools and swamps, the flowers consisted chiefly of tree blooms. At that time, about the middle of September, a tree, something like an ash as to the leaf, burst into bloom. The blooms were like bunches of gigantic buttercups of a brilliant yellow colour. At first we were delighted with them. The golden flowers brought light and colour into our huts, and were admirably set off by the brown walls. But after two or three weeks of yellow it became intolerable. In like manner the scarlet bloom of a species of azalea at first charmed and then wearied. Everything in Africa is excessive—the light, the heat, the vegetation, the wild beasts!

Just at that time the great hunter Mr. Selous came to Umtali. We were much afraid that we should miss him, but he sent us word that he would come as soon as he could get his shirt washed. When we received this message we felt sure he was a delightful person—and our instincts did not deceive us.

Mr. Selous appeared to be a man of about eight-and-thirty, light, active, and giving one an impression of presence of mind and resource. Of his personal appearance it is impossible to remember anything but his eyes, which are extraordinarily clear and limpid.

We persuaded our distinguished guest to tell us some of his adventures, which he did with great charm and modesty. He is known throughout Africa as the man who never tells a lie. If one were to make the most incredible statement, adding, "Selous told me so," people would say, "This is a hard saying, but, if you heard it from Selous, it must be true." What a splendid reputation to have anywhere, but especially in Africa! He told us he had shot twenty-three lions to his own gun, and had helped to put an end to nine others. This was two years ago. We told him about those we had heard roaring around us on the way up, and how frightened we had often been. He said our mode of travelling, sleep-about in the open beside dim fires, was extremely foolhardy, and we should probably have suffered for it had not the country been so well stocked with game. A hungry lion, he added, will jump over any fire, and what he will or will not dare cannot possibly be calculated.

A terrible event which occurred a few miles from the camp, just after Mr. Selous left for Salisbury, gave point to this observation.

Mr. Teal, the same young fellow whose venison I had fried in sardine oil, went out prospecting, taking with him a native servant, a waggon, and a span of oxen, and leaving his brother at home on a farm which the two were beginning to cultivate. The next day the native, beside himself with terror, appeared at the farm, and told the elder Teal that his brother had been devoured by a lion. Snatching up his rifle, and calling to his natives to follow, the distracted man sped away to the spot where his brother's waggon was still outspanned. After a brief search, the head of the unhappy young Teal was found under a bank. Part of his arm was lying close by. The native said that after supping and making up the fire, he and his master rolled themselves in their blankets, and went to sleep under the waggon. Suddenly, not a rustle having betrayed his presence, a lion seized the white man by the foot and dragged him away. The native crept out from under the other end of the waggon, and swarmed up a tree. There, in the bright moonlight, he saw the lion drag his master across the veldt towards a high bank. The lioness sprang out of the grass, and ran after her mate, giving their prey playful taps in true cat-like fashion, and uttering little grunts of pleasure. The native had a rifle, but was too terrified to fire. Had he done so he might have scared the lions, and given his master a chance of escape. As it was, the unhappy man's shrieks were heard for many minutes.

It was, up to that time, the popular belief that a lion will not take a man, if he can get a bullock, and that he prefers a native to a white man. Also that he does not understand waggons, and is afraid of them. This horrible tragedy proved all these theories to be based on nothing.

As soon as this news reached the camp, Mr. Fiennes went out in search of the lions, but found, somewhat to his disappointment, that they had been shot by a Dutchman the night before.

Mr. Selous gave us a huge bundle of newspapers before leaving Umtali, and rifled his waggon to fill our empty store-room. The papers were a great boon. We had had no letters since we left Cape Town in April. English news of any kind seems to bring one nearer home. We sent some letters off by

Mr. Selous, who would take them to Salisbury, and get them sent on as quickly as possible. In these days one can send a letter to Umtali from London in six weeks, but at the time I am writing of, 1891, it often took three weeks to reach Salisbury from Umtali. This will give some idea of the difficulties which the excellent postal organisation, now existing, had to overcome.

Of late we had seen but little of the Bishop. He had gone on an exploring tour to some kraals, with an eye towards future mission stations. Returning to Umtali at the beginning of September, he left almost immediately for Salisbury. The clergyman who was bringing his waggon across the Transvaal had as yet made no sign. The Bishop hoped to get news of him at Salisbury.

The native labour question in Manica was almost as vexed a one as the eight hours' question in England. It was almost impossible to procure boys, and, even when one had succeeded in engaging a few, they promptly fled. In consequence the hospital huts were making no progress.

M'Tassa, the "King" of Manica, was dissatisfied with the present the Chartered Company had given him. He wanted rifles and cartridges, and had only received old uniforms, indifferent limbo, and a few caps. Mr. Fiennes went over to the King's kraal to remonstrate with him about the behaviour of his men, and some of the runaway natives were sent back.

Curiously enough the Bishop, who worked his boys hard and paid them little, was the only person in the country with whom the natives would stay. I think one reason of his success in managing natives lay in the fact that he treated them consistently. His boys were neither playthings nor slaves; were well fed, regularly paid, and cared for when sick.

A native never understands familiarity on the part of his chief. Yet they are so fantastically quaint, that it is difficult to avoid laughing at and with them. More than once we split on this rock, our boys becoming idle and insubordinate. The native, too, believes in the ready money system, and requires to be paid at the very hour or minute his money falls due. He appears with a piece of string, on which he has made a knot for every day he has worked, stretching out his hands for "mali" (money). If the "mali" is not forthcoming that very instant—good-bye to peace! You are followed about the whole day. You drive the man away twenty times; he returns. You send for an interpreter, and explain that gold is coming down in the waggons but has not yet arrived. Fruitless effort! The native only repeats, "Nyanga pelile—funa mali," "The month is finished, I want money."

The Bishop only paid his boys with a blanket, or a stretch or two of limbo, worth perhaps eightpence; very rarely, he told us, did he give money; yet natives swarmed at the Mission Farm. The Chartered Company paid £1 per month in gold, and found it very difficult to procure native labour. Of course the Company's natives had many masters—some were good, others brutal and drunken; drinking was beginning to take very great proportions in Umtali.

It was sad, terrible, yet the men had very many excuses. I do not believe that any community of men, from any part of the world, would have shown to much greater advantage under similar circumstances.

The Umtali-ite of those days had absolutely nothing to do, was without books or papers, and had gone through great hardships. The certainty that it would be more difficult than any one had supposed, to "open up the country," as the phrase went, quickly followed the wild excitement created by the discovery of wonderful gold-reefs. Drinking bars abounded — the Jew traders took care of that. And, in addition to all these causes, there was that terrible African depression, which all who have visited the Dark Continent must experience. It sweeps over a community, as a mist descends from the mountain-tops, and difficult indeed is it to shake it off. Therefore, whilst deploring the fact that two-thirds of the population were at that time almost always drunk, it would be extremely unfair to judge them too harshly. Of course drink increased the difficulties of dealing with the natives, leading as it did to all kinds of ill-treatment. The Mashona never retaliates. If kicked and cuffed, he vanishes in the night, and leaves no trace.

In spite of all delays one hospital hut was nearly finished by the 22nd of September. On that eventful day the waggons which Captain Heany had sent down to Chimoio returned, bringing with them part of our luggage. The whole of Sister Welby's effects were there, and a small box belonging to Sister Lucy. All my possessions and most of hers were lost. We heard that they had been abandoned by one of the Mission men, "somewhere on the veldt." Though the Chartered Company sent two exploring parties to search for the boxes, no trace of them was ever discovered. They were said to have been rifled by natives. To this day the route from 'Mpanda's to Umtali is marked by abandoned waggons, and broken and rotting packing-cases.

These waggons brought with them a rumour to the effect that Mr. Rhodes was on his way from Beira, and would reach Umtali shortly. Nobody believed this at the time. Dr. Jameson, the Administrator, was expected, too, in a few days. We hoped to see him, and have something definitely settled with regard to stores. We could not go on much longer living on public charity, nor could the officers' mess be expected to feed us and the patients. The Mission had no stores to speak of, and the possibility of getting up any more was very doubtful.

On the 26th of September our first patient arrived. It was the last sort of case I should have expected out there, the man being elderly, and apparently in very nearly the last stage of phthisis. With care and good food he might be patched up perhaps, but good food was not to be had. The hospital hut not being ready, our patient brought a tent, which was pitched some little way off, outside our compound. Dr. Lichfield told us to give the old man dinner, of "whatever we had going." As we had nothing going but some stodgy cookies, the sergeants' mess undertook to send up "something," and something did come by and by, in the shape of a huge plateful of not over fresh tinned lobster.

None of the Company's officials, not even the doctor, would take the responsibility of ordering any "hospital comforts," as they are called in Africa. So we took the responsibility on ourselves, feeling sure the Administrator would come to the rescue; and the British South Africa Company's Hospital, Umtali, was opened with furniture and stores consisting of two or three iron spoons, two tin mugs, a couple of pots of Liebig's extract of meat, and a packet of maizena—a species of corn-flour, which, when boiled in milk, the African doctors prefer to arrowroot. It also serves to make excellent blanc-mange, as we discovered when we became a little less stupid about household matters.

Dr. Jameson appeared at Umtali towards the end of September. "Dr. Jim of Mashonaland" was well known to us by reputation, as a brilliant surgeon. Legends of his wonderful operations and cures will long linger at Kimberley. His appearance somewhat disappointed us, but before being in his company five minutes one is struck with his quickness of perception. Scarcely have you begun a sentence, when he knows how it will end. No one sees a point, nor catches an allusion, with more rapidity. Our first interview with our Administrator was not a particularly pleasant one. I am free to confess that we forgot diplomacy, and vented a good deal of pent-up irritation on our visitor's head.

> Mieux persuade,
> Et peut davantage
> Un doux visage
> Qu'un homme armé,

is a truth which no woman should forget!

Unfortunately Dr. Jameson, in the course of conversation, said we had come up a year too early, but that now we had arrived, he must try and find us patients. "Supposing you first find a hospital," was the obvious retort which we did not fail to make. Then, taking Dr. Jameson's speech to imply blame to the Bishop for bringing us up, we proceeded to denounce the muddle of the Chartered Company's affairs, the drink which they allowed to be imported for the sake of revenue, and a great many other things which were absolutely no business of ours. "Jameson went into that hut a man, and came out a mouse," said the officer who brought him to us, and who sat in silent dismay in a corner of the hut.

But the Administrator was much too large-minded to bear malice. Instead of resenting our impolitic reproaches, he revenged himself generously by making every arrangement both for the hospital and for ourselves, which the state of the country permitted. From that date the Chartered Company took entire charge of us, and, as regarded material wants, we had nothing more to do with the Mission. The Administrator authorised us to order all necessaries for hospital and ourselves, and the Company paid the bills without a murmur.

The hospital hut being open we took in three patients, the poor old man in the tent requesting not to be moved. There was no chance now of prolonging his life for any time. Indeed, he died on the 8th of October.

I shall never forget night-nursing in that tent. Sister Lucy and I did it together, as we were each afraid of going up and down the hill alone. The fate of Mr. Teal was in our minds, as we sat by a small fire near the tent, with intense darkness around us, and the cry of a passing hyæna curdling the blood in our veins. When the hut was built we could sit in the porch, the sleeping patients inside were a sort of company, and the night seemed to pass more quickly.

On the day on which our first patient died, the Bishop came to say good-bye. We had hoped his departure for England would have been delayed till December. His clergyman, Mr. Sewell, had not yet arrived. Dr. Knight Bruce himself had only reached Mashonaland in May, and it seemed a short sojourn. The dreaded rainy season was at hand. The whole township and hospital was to be moved to a distance of five miles, its present site being considered unfavourable for the development of a town. Everything was still in an unsettled state. We could not help feeling a little forlorn as we saw the Bishop ride away. However, he explained that it was absolutely necessary, in the interests of the Mission, that he should go to England and collect money. Of course, the interests of the Mission came before everything. Nothing more could be said.

The very day that he left, Mr. Rhodes arrived. He did not stay in the Police Camp, but accepted the hospitality offered by Captain Heany. He was besieged with petitions of all sorts. Malcontents and chronic grumblers went to his hut, and came away in a few moments cheerful and satisfied.

Not that anything was altered in the condition of affairs—the man's mere personal magnetism wrought the change.

The Premier's stay was not to exceed two days, so we did not expect to see him. Great was our astonishment, when, on the morning of Saturday, the 10th of October, one of the officials rushed breathless to our hut with the information that Mr. Rhodes was coming to see us. This man was the only official who had been persistently unpleasant, and he had come to request that we would let bygones be bygones! His experience of women must have been a sad one, for we heard that he really believed we should try and revenge ourselves by complaining to Mr. Rhodes of his behaviour to us.

As we were leaving the hospital hut, Mr. Rhodes rode up alone. His appearance and Roman Emperor type of head are too well known to need description. We took him into the hut, knowing our patients would like to see him. It was not without difficulty that we persuaded him to enter. He said that if he were ill himself he should not like a stranger to come and look at him. But when we told him that the patients would be greatly disappointed if they did not see him, he yielded at once. He must have thought them rather stupid. They stared with all the powers of their eyes, but said nothing. We discovered afterwards that they could not understand his not having finer clothes. I think they expected a more gorgeous apparition, a chain and ring man probably, suggestive of De Beers Mine.

As soon as Mr. Rhodes was seated on a box in our hut, he asked for pen and ink, saying he would give us a cheque at once for the hospital. How much would we have? Would £100 do? Amply, we said. Well, he thought he had better make it £150. I feel sure that if we had clamoured for £500, he would have given it. His generosity is proverbial, everything about the man is big —faults, virtues, projects. His ambition itself is largely tinctured with altruism. He is the darling of Fortune—and that blind goddess does not often select her favourites from the Sunday School. We were especially charmed by the great man's simple manners, and boyish enjoyment of a joke. He told us that he had made political capital out of our walk up. The Cape Town Government having objected to his journey to Umtali on the score of danger, he had answered that if ladies had been able to walk up without tents or waggons, it would be absurd for a man not to be afraid to ride up, as the horses, of course, would fall victims to the fly! After this statement he had met with no further opposition.

Mr. Rhodes remained, chatting delightfully, for a couple of hours, and left promising to see us through all our difficulties. Nor was this a vain promise. Of his many kindnesses, we thought most of his having remembered to replace the small medical library, which had been lost with our luggage. The books not being procurable at the Cape, this busy man took the trouble of having them sent for to England. He left that evening for Salisbury, leaving every one as hopeful, enterprising, and confident in the resources of the country, as they had been dispirited and pessimistic before his arrival.

Captain Heyman, of Masse-Kesse fame, had left Mashonaland some weeks before, and one of his officers took his place pending the arrival of Captain Turner, of the Scots, to whom the appointment of officer in command and resident magistrate had been given. Captain Turner was a tall, soldierly young fellow, with a splendid physique. It would have seemed almost impossible, then, to believe that in less than a year he would have fallen a victim to the fever-fiend.

After Mr. Rhodes's departure the work of starting New Umtali began in earnest. Mr. Fiennes, with some of his police and a number of natives, encamped over at the new site, and set to work building the police camp, together with our huts and the hospital. This last was quite a stately square building, with a small operation room in the centre and a ward on either side; the whole being capable of holding from twenty to thirty sick.

Some sort of change was indeed necessary. The rains had begun; the existing hospital hut was an awful place. Hardly a square inch of roof was water-tight. We put up an umbrella here, hung a waterproof sheet there, and did what was possible. But it remained a cheerless, uncomfortable abode; and it went to one's heart to see a sick man lying in such a place. As to our own huts, they were past any attempt at patching. We huddled together in the centre of one, where there was a dry space of about a yard square, all the rest being a sort of swamp. However, the rain was not continuous. A few hours' sun dried up everything. Things might have been worse, and were improving rapidly.

One Sunday afternoon some interesting visitors appeared at the door of our hut. They were Mr. and Mrs. Bent, accompanied by a Mr. Swan. We had hardly shaken hands, when Mrs. Bent asked us what we thought of her dress. This was a difficult question to answer. Mrs. Bent's costume consisted of an ordinary print blouse, worn over obvious stays; a woollen kilt, reaching to just below her knees; knickerbockers; top boots; and a pith helmet, which gave its wearer something of the air of a Britannia who had exchanged the rest of her garments with a scarecrow! We gently suggested that if the fair explorer had consulted Redfern, or, better still, Martin of Dublin, either would have built her something much more workmanlike and beguiling. After this Mrs. Bent made herself very pleasant, showed us photographs which she had taken with much skill, a talent which was no doubt of great use to her husband. Mr. Bent might have been the "Silent Member" himself, he spoke so little; but, the next day, when we went to his encampment, he showed us his sketch-books, and was much less mute. He was fresh from those strange Mashonaland ruins which have given rise to so much conjecture. Mr. Bent supposed them to be extremely ancient. He told us that, without consulting the archives at Lisbon, he could not give a decided opinion on their origin. At that time he seemed to believe them to be the ruins of a temple and fortress. There, he thought, weird rights had been solemnised and fierce battles fought.

Mr. Selous differed entirely from this view. He believes the ruins to be comparatively modern, and the remains of native work. There is a tradition that a great chief is buried under them, and Mashonas still go and worship there. Mr. Selous is probably the best authority on the subject, knowing Africa as thoroughly as he does, and being able to converse with the native as easily as with an Englishman, whilst Mr. Bent could neither speak nor understand the language. But Mr. Bent appeared certain that the Portuguese only could throw light on the problem. He said that the Portuguese had certainly been all over the country, and that a Portuguese archæologist who would devote himself to the subject would find the archives of Lisbon, and very likely of other old cities, rich in most interesting materials.

A few days later the Bents rode away to Masse-Kesse, *en route* for the coast. We saw them go, with something of a pang. They would probably be our last visitors. When the rainy season set in thoroughly, Umtali would be like a besieged city, and its inhabitants cut off from all communication with the outer world.

CHAPTER VII

Leaving Old for New Umtali—Our Malay boy Jonosso—
"Your Excellency's plate"—Rain—Waiting for the
waggon—An accident—Water-tight huts—Furnishing
the hospital—Sister Lucy as carpenter—The white
prisoner—His thumbs tied—Algernon Caulfield makes
an arm-chair—Illness and departure of Eustace
Fiennes—Sister B. Welby and Dr. Lichfield—Arrival
of our clergyman—His strange attire—His disputes
with the mission workers—He "chucks his orders"—
Advent of a professional baker—Sister Lucy's cake—Its
effect on Col. Pennefather—Wedding cake—The first
marriage in Manica—Keeping Christmas—The police
deputation—The cow—Sports—Magistrate and Civil
Commissioner "on the burst"—All the police arrest
each other—The last man—General amnesty—The
Colonel again— "Order of the Sack"—Good-byes.

In December, 1891, we took possession of our new hospital. It stood on a gentle eminence surrounded by trees, commanding a fine view of the plain on which the future township was to be built. Rocky hills closed in the valley. On one of these lived

M'Tassa, the Manica king. Behind the hospital were our huts. At the back of these the compound sloped upward, losing itself in a thickly wooded hill. It was a pretty place; the rocks, broken ground, and trees, giving it a very picturesque air.

The journey from Old to New Umtali, a distance of about six miles, assumed quite the proportions of an expedition. What we called "our furniture," such rattle-traps as would be disdained by an East-end flitter, was piled up on a bullock waggon. Having seen that the pots and pans were firmly bound to the waggon with reims—that is, long strips of dried cow-hide—we walked off, the natives setting fire to the huts as we left them.

We had been so fortunate as to come across a wandering Malay from the coast. Malays make the best servants, they are so spotlessly clean. Our boy's name was "Jonosso." He was much too important and dignified a person to have anything to do with the waggon. "Where," he said to me in Portuguese, "Where does your Excellency wish your Excellency's plate to be packed?" Our "plate" consisted of six little tea-spoons which we had brought up with us, and a few steel forks of the cheapest description. All were kept in an empty biscuit-tin, as sacred to Jonosso as the most splendid plate-chest to an English butler. He stalked before us bearing it on his head—a strange figure in a long blue shirt, or rather night-gown, reaching to the middle of his calves; white and scarlet striped trousers of thin muslin; a scarlet fez on his woolly head;[1] and a perpetual curl of smoke issuing from his lips.

Following him as quickly as we could, for the day looked threatening, we reached New Umtali towards noon. Hardly had we taken refuge in Mr. Fiennes's hut, when the rain began. In a few moments the huts appeared to be standing in a sort of lagoon. The earth is so dry and hard in Africa, that the

---

[1] The "Malays" in Africa generally have woolly heads, probably being of mixed race.

rain does not sink into it for a long time. Not till one has lived in these climates, does one understand the force of the Biblical expression, "the heavens opened."

Meanwhile, there we sat, watching the rain, and wishing the waggon would come. Hour after hour passed. At last a boy was despatched to see what had happened. He soon returned, saying the waggon had broken down. Off rode Mr. Fiennes and his men, and by their united efforts the waggon was patched up, and reached its destination an hour after dark.

Everything had been upset in a "donga" or deep ditch between two hills. The rains had filled the "donga" with water. Our tea had turned into a sort of soup, our meal into dough. The precious packing-cases, on which a heavy man could sit without fear of accident, were smashed, and only fit for firewood. Our blankets were happily dry. We had a fire lit in the little kitchen hut; spread waterproofs on the floor; and, rolled in our rugs, slept soundly till morning. The rain poured all night, but none found its way through the thatch. The certainty of having water-tight huts consoled us for the misadventures of our flitting.

The next day was devoted to getting huts and hospital into something like order. After a great deal of trouble, and after taking Mr. Rhodes's name in vain a hundred times a day, we succeeded in obtaining fairly comfortable canvas stretchers for the patients, instead of the horrible grass and sticks which had furnished the former hospital hut. This was something. The musty smell of grass which has served for some time as a bed, the impossibility of changing it, the swarms of fleas which it harbours, make it the very last thing which ought to be used for sick people. As soon as the sun has thoroughly dried the land after the rains, settlers set fire to the long dry grass. It is dangerous to live in the midst of it, as a chance spark will set it on fire, and a whole encampment be swept away in a few moments. So that except at one time of the year, there is great difficulty in obtaining grass for thatching and other purposes.

Had it not been for these canvas stretchers the hospital would have been absolutely empty. It was necessary to have a few tables. Sister Lucy, who had a great turn for carpentering, set to work to make some. It was amusing to see her hammering and sawing, with the air of a professional carpenter. Our little black boys took a lively interest in these operations. Like Dora Copperfield and her pens, they felt they were helped largely if they held the nails, or passed the saw.

We soon obtained other assistance, however, in the shape of a white prisoner. This man, a Bavarian prospector, shot at a native and shattered his leg. The boy had followed his master about, clamouring for his money. In a moment of irritation, the latter snatched up his gun, and discharged it at the boy. Dr. Lichfield rode out to the German's camp, and amputated the injured leg, the boy eventually recovering.

Our prisoner, who paid a fine, and had to do three months' hard labour, was marched to the hospital compound every morning. He wore the usual flannel shirt and miner's trousers, but large green arrows were painted all over them. The sun melted the paint, which ran down him in every direction, and wherever he stood he left a little green pool.

There was no door to the gaol, so the Resident Magistrate, a man of resource, had the prisoner's thumbs tied behind him at night. The German, accustomed to a paternal government, submitted; but when it came to tying Englishmen's thumbs, a disturbance was made, and the practice had to be dropped.

The German was not Sister Lucy's only aide-de-camp. Mr. Algernon Caulfield, a nice long-legged English boy, who had just abandoned diplomacy at the Hague in favour of an unsophisticated life in Mashonaland, offered his services. He could actually turn a packing-case into an arm-chair in a few hours.

When covered with turkey twill, the *ci-devant* box appeared to have come from Maple's. It was always pushed into a prominent position in the hut, and invariably excited the liveliest admiration and envy.

Mr. Seymour-Fort, whose camp was a few miles from New Umtali, became a frequent visitor at the hospital. It was well for us that these excellent friends were at hand. The Bishop had left, so had Mr. Campion; and now Mr. Fiennes, to whom we owed so much, whose help we counted on in all difficulties—and never in vain—was going also. His health had broken down; it was necessary that he should escape to the colony, if not to England, before the Beira route became impracticable. We saw him leave with a regret which may be imagined.

Meanwhile, an event was approaching, in which the whole of the little colony took much interest. Sister B. Welby and Dr. Lichfield were about to be married.

We offered no opposition to the marriage,

although feeling that the work would fall somewhat heavily on two. But Sister B. Welby detested African nursing, and could not accommodate herself to the makeshift arrangements, the perpetual cooking and cleaning. Unable to make herself happy in the hospital, it was much better she should leave it, since an opportunity offered. A person who takes life too seriously in a pioneer hospital, who can extract no fun from the odd contrivances one has recourse to, and the many inevitable difficulties, must obviously be very unhappy. Only cheery souls should attempt African nursing. For these reasons the marriage was fixed for Christmas Eve. We had then been but four months in Manica, and our work was only beginning, so Sister B. Welby escaped the worst of the hardship and drudgery in store for us.

The long-expected clergyman had arrived some weeks before we left Old Umtali. I must say that the appearance of this gentleman, whose name was Sewell, was a great shock to us. He wore a helmet; a flannel shirt; and coarse blue trousers, much too short, of the type dear to navvies. These were held in place by a large scarlet handkerchief, which however did its work so indifferently that Mr. Sewell was always hitching up his trousers like a comic sailor in a pantomime. Anything more unclerical than his manners and get-up cannot be imagined.

His first visit was entirely taken up with complaints of his position and of the other mission workers. He said he had no money. Like Dr. Glanville he possessed but £2! He also informed us that the Bishop had left him no authority, excepting over souls. A mere boy was in charge of stores and work. He was not going to stand it; he would work his way home before the mast. We tried to persuade the irate clergyman that the cure of souls was the only important part of the Mission. For a long time he would do nothing but rage against the place, people, and Bishop. "Am I to depend for a pound of butter on an office boy?" he cried, over and over again. After talking for an hour or so, he was at last somewhat appeased. He consented to write to Dr. Knight Bruce, and remain quietly at Umtali until he received an answer. Practically this meant remaining till the end of the rainy season, as he could not hear from the Bishop till it would be too late to attempt leaving the country. With this we were satisfied. The delay would give the Bishop time to remedy the situation. I may state here that, the following Easter, Mr. Sewell, to use his own expression, "chucked his orders," and went into partnership with a Jew tavern-keeper. Poor Bishop! he told us the man had been most highly recommended to him. Surely people who give unfounded recommendations have a very false idea of what charity really means.

Meanwhile the resources of the country were increasing. Imagine our joy when a real baker came from Salisbury, and we realised that the days of amateur bread-making were past and done with. Of all our difficulties I really think this was the worst. We took infinite pains, and consulted the best local authorities,—but what would come out of that baking pot was always the merest lottery. I remember once receiving a present of currants, upon which Sister Lucy resolved to make a currant cake. In the pride of our hearts we boasted of our great doings, with the result that Colonel Pennefather and two or three of his officers came over to tea.

Alas! in some mysterious way, the cake had turned into a sort of plum pudding! Sister Lucy was, however, equal to the occasion; she fried the pudding, and served large slices of it to our guests. The Colonel ate his slice like a man, and a very polite one. We heard that he was very irritable for the next twenty-four hours, only recovering when rumours of a lion were brought into camp. Irritable or not, every one liked the Colonel. We always looked forward to his visits, and were very sorry when he left Mashonaland.

Of course we could eat fried lumps of dough, even though it was not very wholesome. Bread for the hospital was the difficulty. Though we often made excellent loaves, and naturally improved daily, results were never certain. The first day the baker's boy left a batch of bread at the hospital was, therefore, a red-letter day. We immediately ordered a wedding cake for Christmas Eve. It could not be iced, but it would be a real cake.

Early on the morning of the 24th of December, Sister Lucy and I went forth to hunt for flowers. Climbing a steep hill about two miles distant we found a mass of Cape jasmine, and returned laden with the spoil. These flowers filled the huts with exquisite perfume, and lent something of poetry to the rude surroundings.

The marriage took place at four in the afternoon, in a hut which we had draped with blue and white limbo for the occasion. Mr. Sewell officiated; the Resident Magistrate gave the bride away.

Dr. Lichfield looked quite smart in a new Karkee suit, and Mrs. Lichfield extremely nice in a white serge uniform frock. Most fortunately, none of her luggage had been lost on its way from the coast.

After the ceremony the party adjourned to another hut, and partook of tea in tin mugs. The cake never appeared. The baker was keeping Christmas! Then the Doctor and his bride walked across to the township, where he had put up a few picturesque huts, which Mrs. Lichfield decorated very prettily.

Christmas Day dawned on an already excited community. I do not think it is exaggerating to say that by noon every one in the place, with the exception of three or four men, was very tipsy indeed.

A deputation of police came to wish us a "Merry Christmas." They confided to us that they were great scamps, but would always stand by us. "If a civilian looksh atsh you, Sistersh, you justsh sendsh to ush," exclaimed these excellent fellows, propping themselves up against the hut. We thanked them, and watched them striding away, in long curves, to the camp. Presently they returned. They wished to present us with a cow,—would we do them the favour of accepting? We would—with pleasure. We had patients in hospital, and had not yet bought any cows. Milk would be a great boon. Thereupon they retired, this time taking a decidedly zig-zag course. No cow, however, appeared; and, to our great amusement, we heard that the "deputation" had stolen a cow for us. I think the animal had strayed into the camp. As our friends were driving it to the hospital, the infuriated owner swooped down on them, routed the gallant but unsteady police, and carried off his cow in triumph. Perhaps the generosity of our friends was somewhat misplaced, but they were kindly souls.

Christmas Day was devoted to sports of various kinds; but, before the afternoon was far spent, the good-natured stage of drunkenness was replaced by the quarrelsome one.

A free fight took place round the too-well-supplied refreshment waggon. The Civil Commissioner announced his intention of tearing the Resident Magistrate, who was also Officer in Command, from his horse. This official ordered the Civil Commissioner to be arrested. Friends of the latter declared that no one but the Administrator had power to do so. Nevertheless he was arrested, and whirled across the plain, to the Police Camp. Were his thumbs to be tied? That was the great question. Meanwhile the Magistrate suspended the Civil Commissioner from his functions. He in his turn suspended the Magistrate. Hubbub and confusion followed. Before midnight all the police were under arrest, we were told—the last man having provoked his punishment by holding a candle crooked, whilst the Magistrate himself tied the thumbs of some of his prisoners!

Next day all was forgotten and forgiven. At a banquet, followed by a smoking concert, the Civil Commissioner and the Magistrate drank each others' healths. Each man swore that the other was the best fellow he had ever met. Till the end of the year, says my diary, camp and township remained "on the burst."

No attempt at holding service having been made, we wrote to Mr. Sewell offering him the hospital till he could have a church-hut erected. He came to see us, making a more favourable impression than at his first visit, and it was settled that he should hold a service on New Year's Eve, and regularly every Sunday. He talked quite earnestly about his endeavours to do good, and very likely he was in earnest. He preached well, having much command of language; and, had he chosen, he might have been a great influence for good in Umtali.

On the 2nd of January, 1892, Colonel Pennefather rode into the camp. Every one rejoiced to see him. He told us he projected spending the rainy season in Manica, and set to work at once to make his hut comfortable. Great, therefore, was the general surprise, when, on the 4th of January, a runner brought him a dispatch informing him that the Military Police were to be disbanded, and a Civil Police created. The Colonel's services would, therefore, no longer be required. He could rejoin his regiment when he pleased. In point of fact the Company was retrenching in all directions. A Civil Government had been established. The Military Police were considered both expensive and unnecessary.

The announcement was too sudden not to be unpleasant, but the Colonel took the affair very calmly. "I've received the Order of the Sack, Sister." That was all he said about it. We were very sorry indeed to say good-bye to him. We had hoped that, besides keeping camp and township in order, he would prove a pleasant neighbour. However there was no help for it. Needs must when a retrenching Administrator drives.

CHAPTER VIII

The hospital — Patients — Work — Contrivances — Project of brick hospital — Poultry yard — Capricious hens — Mashona cows — The bread question — Our baker — Attempts to bake himself — A breadless community — Montague Bowden — His last game of cricket — His illness and death — Scaring off wild beasts — The funeral — Our dispenser "on the burst" — Opium poisoning — Dispenser attempts suicide — Imprisoned — Our protest — Dispenser dismissed — Illness of Sister Lucy — Flight of natives — A terrible week — Drink — An extraordinary bill — Departure of magistrate — The reign of Law in Manica — Birth of first English child in Mashonaland — Serious illness of Mrs. Tulloch — Our huts burnt to the ground — Narrow escape of Mrs. Tulloch — A tipsy fire brigade — Generosity — Arrival of Dr. Matthew Johnston — Our patient saved — Christening of Cecil Rhodes Tulloch — He leaves the hospital in triumph.

THE hospital was soon in working order, and rarely without patients. Indeed from January to September, it was never empty for a day. Referring to my diary, I see that from the middle of January till nearly the end of March, we left the hospital compound once only. Or in English nursing parlance, we had one afternoon off duty.

It was the unbroken continuity of work which made it trying, rather than its arduous nature. The native servants were most uncertain. They came and went at their own caprice. Sometimes we had a good staff, sometimes only one boy for everything. In no case was it safe to send even a cup of milk over to the hospital by a native. He was pretty sure to give it to the wrong person.

Some of the cases were slight, chiefly requiring rest in bed and good food; others were brought in from the Veldt in a serious condition, and demanded constant attention. When these more serious cases were in hospital, we took it in turns to remain for twenty-four hours on duty. Tiring as this was, we found it answered better than if one of us had remained on night duty, and the other on day. What with cooking, nursing, and the general superintendence of the natives, the work involved in keeping huts, hospital, and compound in a state of spotless cleanliness was considerable. One Sister on day duty would have had to work without pause from six in the morning till night time. Hard work soon tells on women and men in a tropical climate. However we both had excellent health, were both really fond of nursing, and did not grudge the hard work.

Little by little the great barn, dignified by the name of "hospital" became, considering the circumstances, a comfortable retreat. Sister Lucy made some capital wooden trays out of packing-cases. Our white linen aprons were useless, for we had no time to starch and iron. Indeed, there was no starch to be had. We, therefore, converted them into napkins for the hospital trays. By means of these contrivances we were able to serve the patients' food, such as it was, nicely enough. Every one knows that the manner in which nourishment is offered to a sick man is very nearly as important as the food itself. I think our trays, rude as they were, with their white napkins and little bunches of flowers, often tempted a patient to eat, and so gave him a first impulse towards recovery.

We were lucky enough to secure a number of Italian silk rugs from a trader, who had brought them to Mashonaland, "on spec" as he said. They served as quilts, and their bright colours gave the wards a very cheery air. When we had covered the mud walls with the pale primrose-coloured native mats, and had obtained brick floors, and cupboards for blankets, dressings, and sundries, we felt we could do little more to the place. It was then that we turned our attentions to collecting money for the creation of a brick hospital.

We had bought cows, and started a

poultry yard. The hospital was, therefore, plentifully supplied with milk, eggs, and fowls. The fowls proved very troublesome. A Mashona hen is a thoroughly undisciplined bird. She lays her tiny eggs in a rush, and then refuses to lay for weeks. If you keep her shut up, however large the enclosure, you will not get an egg. If you let her run free, she lays in the most inconvenient places—preferably in one's bed. Therefore, as soon as one or two neighbours started poultry farms, we gave up our fowls.

It was some time, too, before we could manage our cows. The breed in Mashonaland is small and very pretty, not unlike the Kerry cow. But what a difference in disposition! The Mashona cow refuses to give any milk, unless she is first allowed to feed her calf for a few moments. The calf is then dragged away and held under the cow's nose, whilst a native milks hurriedly. For a short time the cow appears unaware of what is going on. Then suddenly the milk ceases.

The calf is again had recourse to, and is again torn away. So it goes on till a certain amount of milk is obtained. Milking is thus a long process, involving great noise, lowings, and shoutings. Sometimes cow and calf burst their bonds and escape, with a crowd of yelling natives after them. A very good cow gives twelve pints of milk a day. Such a milker is indeed a treasure. From six to eight pints is the usual quantity obtained. We left the hospital in possession of a herd of ten beautiful cows. It gave one a delightful homelike feeling to see them driven up from the pastures in the evening. One or two of them were great favourites, and would trot up to have their heads scratched, and get a crust of bread.

Though Umtali owned a baker, and there were moments when he sold very good little cakes, yet we were never quite sure whether he was going to send any bread or not. For a long time it came at all sorts of hours and in all sorts of conditions. Having asked one day why there were so many pebbles in the loaves, I was told that it was owing to the baker's method of kneading his dough. Being generally "on the burst," he had great difficulty in mixing his flour. When it was ready for kneading, he would think he saw masses of dough all round him. Then, after making rushes in every direction, and failing to grasp anything solid, he would pull himself together, and dash at his table, falling presently with a clash into the dough, and rolling with it on the floor. One day, the story goes, he tried to bake himself in his own oven. His natives pulled him out, and put him to bed. They did not see that the dough was in bed before him, so the next day Manica was breadless. Such tales are very likely to have been exaggerated. I tell them as they were told to me. They are certainly strictly in character and true to local colour.

To return to the hospital. Our day was mapped out as follows. At six o'clock one of us called the natives, had fires lit and tea made, served round the early tea to the patients, and saw the hospital boy start sweeping. For a long time we had no brooms, but used branches of a sort of aromatic shrub, which left a pleasant fresh smell. Then the beds were made, blankets put out in the sun, bed tables scrubbed, temperatures taken, medicines given, and the patients washed. Meanwhile, whichever of us was not taking the hospital work that morning went to the kitchen, saw it thoroughly cleaned, and had all the water-buckets filled for the day. Then the patients' trays were put ready, and their breakfasts prepared. These were sent over to the hospital at about a quarter to eight. First the full diets, generally consisting of porridge, coffee, or tea, toast, eggs or rissoles, which we manufactured fairly successfully. Then the light diets were sent over. Cases on liquid diet were fed in small quantities, and often, night and day of course. After the hospital breakfast was served, ours was cooked. Then we saw to the washing up of all the things, the sweeping of our huts and the compound, sent for the meat, and prepared for dinner. Between ten and eleven the doctor went round, and, after his visit, there were often, of course, fresh medicines, lotions, and so on, to be attended to. At eleven the patients had luncheon—beef-tea or milk—and there were generally a good many odds and ends to do, as nursing does not consist only in running round and serving medicines or food. Then came temperatures and medicines again. At half-past twelve there was dinner, followed by our luncheon. Then the patients had a small wash, and generally went to sleep. The natives were very slow about washing up, so we took it in turns to watch them clean and put everything tidily away. Unless there were bad cases in hospital there was generally a respite till half-past three, when the blankets were taken in out of the sun, and put away. Then came medicine and temperatures again, and tea, and, after that, the doctor went round. When our tea was finished, the patients' beds were re-made. Supper followed. We had ours as soon after as possible. When this repast was finished, one of us saw to everything being washed and put away; while the other went over to the hospital, took temperatures, gave medicines, supplied drinks for the night, and made every one as comfortable as possible. If the cases were not severe, and did not require attention at night, we did not sit up. A native slept within, in the small middle room between the two wards, in case of an emergency. This was the routine, which lasted without a break from January, 1892, to September, 1892. It was somewhat varied by bad cases, which could not be left night or day; and by the disappearance of natives, which obliged one to do the cleaning instead of seeing that it was done; but on the whole it was continuous.

In September, 1892, we obtained a cook, which lightened the work much, and gave us some leisure. By this time, too, contact with white men had much improved the boys, and they became more like those to be met with in Kimberley and Johannesburg. If they were taught their work they would begin it, and go on with it without continual following up. Every month of the last six months we spent at Umtali made the conditions of life easier, and we were able to leave the incoming nurses in comparatively comfortable surroundings.

The first case we lost in New Umtali was Mr. Montague Bowden, the well-known cricketer. He was singularly handsome, popular, and with every chance of success in trading and prospecting enterprises.

In February 1892 Mr. Bowden, while travelling from Salisbury to Umtali, was thrown from his cart, but was apparently uninjured. The day after his arrival he played in a cricket match, and it was observed that he was in bad form. The next day but one he had an epileptic seizure, and was conveyed to the hospital. His temperature rose to 107, and he passed away very peacefully on the fourth day after his admittance. On account of the heat it was necessary to keep the doors and windows of the room, where he lay, wide open, and a man with a loaded revolver sat there all night to protect the corpse from wild beasts.

Next day he was buried, the whole community attending his funeral. With great difficulty, owing to the scarcity of wood, a coffin had been made out of whisky cases. It was covered with dark blue limbo. A card, bearing his name and age, was nailed to the lid. Beneath it we placed a large cross of flowers. The remains were carried across the compound to a bullock-cart, and the melancholy procession started. We lingered to watch it wind across the plain, until it disappeared from view, and then with sad steps returned to the wards.

Almost immediately after Mr. Bowden's death a great disturbance was caused by the behaviour of our dispenser. He had been "on the burst" more or less ever since Christmas, and took to giving out medicines without measuring them. One of the patients was taking powders which contained a certain amount of opium, and, after swallowing two or three of these powders, he began to show symptoms which seemed to point to opium poisoning. Suspecting what had happened, we had the powders re-weighed, and found he was taking nearly four times the quantity of opium prescribed in each dose. The doctor was hurriedly sent for. He said there was no doubt about the patient's symptoms, and ordered the usual antidotes to be employed. The Magistrate then appeared on the scene.

Hearing what he had done, the dispenser seized a bottle of laudanum, and fled towards the river. After him went the Magistrate and his myrmidons, recruiting several amateur police on the way. The dispenser had a considerable start, however, the grass was already long, the chase promised to be exciting. Would he have swallowed the poison before they could reach him? Useless fears! The fugitive had carried off not only a phial of laudanum, but a bottle of whisky. When he was caught the phial was full, the bottle empty! He was marched to the camp, and lodged in gaol; native policemen with levelled rifles watched him night and day. Finally, he was released, and requested "not to try it on again."

Of course he ceased to be the hospital dispenser. I say "of course," but probably, if we had not made a stand, he would have been reinstated in his dispensary. Hearing that there was some question of it, we sent the Magistrate a formal declaration to the effect that we must refuse to administer medicines prepared by this man. The matter was referred to the Administrator, and a great inquiry followed. About a hundred and fifty sheets of foolscap, covered with affirmations and declarations, came and went between Fort Salisbury and Umtali, and in the end the dispenser was dismissed.

A month or two later Dr. Lichfield left. He is now district surgeon at Victoria. Dr. Matthew Johnston from St. Bartholomew's took his place.

Before this change was effected, however,

I nearly lost Sister Lucy. She fell ill in March; that same day all our natives fled. I had one little boy, eight years of age, to do everything. There were only six cases in hospital, but four were desperately bad, and two were convalescents, just beginning to be ravenous.

From five in the morning till ten at night I was unceasingly at work, going from Sister Lucy to the hospital, thence to the kitchen. There was no idea of going to bed. Sister Lucy was much too ill for that. I had a white man sitting up in the hospital, but it was necessary to go across continually. The police volunteered their help when Sister Lucy got worse, and kindly undertook the kitchen work, which was an immense help.

I cannot describe the anxiety of that week, it was like an evil dream to look back upon. I lost one patient, a fever case, with bad complications.

Sister Lucy never had a very high temperature; her fever took the form of constant vomiting and tendency to collapse. She used to say that the worst part of it all was when she was a little better. She could not reconcile herself to being in bed, whilst she heard the sound of my steps, backwards and forwards, all day long. The heat, too, was burning—the sun actually seemed to sting as it touched one. It is these first hot days, when the rains are nearly over, that bring the worst phases of fever. However, Sister Lucy happily recovered, and was soon able to take her share of the work.

About this time we lost another patient. He was brought in unconscious after a tremendous "burst." He died after a succession of the most terrible epileptiform attacks I have ever seen. When his affairs were examined, it was found that out of a bill to the amount of £50, £39 were due for whisky!

The Resident Magistrate, one of the kindest and best fellows in the world, now left Umtali. He was replaced by another man, the third who had governed Manica in our short experience.

The new Magistrate was a business-like person. At first we were afraid that he too was tarred with the usual Umtali brush, as his hand shook so much that he could not hold a tea-cup steadily.

We were mistaken. With his advent began the reign of law and order. Regular hours for the opening and shutting of bars were established. Between its periodical "bursts," the township enjoyed long intervals of sobriety. Perhaps for a week at a time not a case of drunkenness would occur, and in proportion to the decrease of drink, so did the fever diminish, without, however, entirely dying out.

Civilisation now began to make progress in Mashonaland, the stores were well supplied, creature comforts were plentiful. The projected railway from Beira to Umtali was much talked of. We were assured that when we left Umtali in 1893, we should depart in the train, and to a certain extent this prediction was verified.

Meanwhile an interesting event occurred.

The first English baby was born in Mashonaland. Mrs. Tulloch, the plucky wife of a prospector, had had herself, as has been already mentioned, and two children carried up in machilas from the coast. She arrived whilst we were still in Old Umtali, and had but lately come over to the new township.

We offered her the use of one of our huts for the confinement, but she preferred remaining at home, and Dr. and Mrs. Lichfield undertook to look after her. The very day the child was born, Mr. Tulloch was carried into hospital in a semi-delirious state. We had several patients in hospital at the time, but, had we imagined that the poor mother would have been left alone all night, one of us would certainly have gone to her. As it was, she spent the whole of that night alone with her children, and a native boy, who fled before morning. A native woman from the coast, obtained with much difficulty, was also there, but stupid with drink. The hut had no door, and was at some distance from neighbours.

Bad symptoms set in during the night. In the morning when the doctor called, he found, to his horror, that a number of wild natives had entered the hut, and were sitting round the patient's bed clamouring for her to trade. He very quickly got rid of them, but Mrs. Tulloch was in a high fever. It was urgent to remove her to the hospital, so we hurriedly prepared a hut for her reception, and sent the ambulance to fetch her. She was in a critical condition, and we had little hope of saving her.

One wild, windy evening, as we were attending to her, a gust of wind tore out the limbo that was nailed over the window, and sent it fluttering into the candle. In less time than it takes to describe, the whole hut was in a blaze. A straw from the roof had caught fire, and long ladders of flame ran up the thatch. We tried to tear it down, to throw up water—in vain. Sister Lucy ran to the dispenser's hut, where Mr. Tulloch happened to be dining. I remained with his wife.

Meanwhile burning thatch began to fall into the hut. Plucky as she was, I feared Mrs. Tulloch would lose her presence of mind, and jump out of bed. Wrapping a blanket round her, I carried her to the door, and soon had the satisfaction of seeing her husband carry her over to the hospital, where there was an empty ward.

All our huts caught fire, and the flames lit up the whole valley. Magistrate and police rushed over from the camp, tore down the blazing thatch, and saved what things they could from the general destruction. The whole of Umtali, in fact, precipitated itself from the township to the hospital.

The men were eager to help, but were hardly in a condition to be of much use. In a burst of zeal one man rushed to the river, a third of a mile away, and fetched a bucket of water. Just as he reached the hospital, he tumbled head over heels, giving himself a thorough drenching. Then, cooled and sobered, he retired to bed, and was heard of no more. One of the guardians of law and order dropped a bottle of whisky as he lurched across the compound. On this the doctor pounced, declaring it forfeited to the hospital. Other men piled the thatch back on the fire, and nearly burnt down the hospital. One man, at the peril of his life, rushed into the burning hut, shouting, " Down, flames; I command you to go out." He was promptly dragged out, and marched off to prison, where, I heard, he complained bitterly of the green spiders and other abnormal reptiles.

With great difficulty the kitchen was saved. We had the sweetest little black-faced monkey. It went quite mad with fright, and bit me badly as I carried it out of the kitchen, and we had to keep it in the dark for a whole day, before its nerves recovered from the shock. At last we got the compound clear, and arranged ourselves as best we could in the hospital. I must not forget to say, that when the men got back to the township, they sent us over everything they could think of that might be of any use. People may be very foolish and tipsy in a pioneer camp, but they are also very generous and warm-hearted—qualities which cover a multitude of sins.

For a few days after this excitement, Mrs. Tulloch appeared to improve, but then she became worse than ever. For eleven days and nights, Sister Lucy and I never rested for more than an hour or so at a time. One had the baby, the other took the mother. Very naturally, the baby, after the first few days, was a perfect little demon of fretfulness. In the midst of our anxiety, Dr. Johnston, from Salisbury, came to replace Dr. Lichfield. He never expected to pull our patient through, but eventually succeeded in doing so.

Seven weeks after his birth, "Cecil Rhodes Tulloch" was christened in one of our newly built huts by Canon Balfour, who at this time came for a few days to Umtali. After the ceremony Mrs. Tulloch was borne away in a machila; a small boy carrying the newly made Christian. A baby's bottle had been improvised out of a pickle bottle, and a glass tube run through a cork. This the natives concluded to be something very precious. One boy headed the march, holding it aloft. Thus, borne away in triumphant procession, the baby which had tyrannised over us for so long vanished out of our lives for ever.

CHAPTER IX

A free day—A visit to Chiconga—Climbing a kopje—The kraal—Gungunyama's raids—The council hut—The chieftainess and her "warriors"—Her answer to the Bishop—We trade—Fashion amongst natives—A blind Lovelace—Instance of ferocity—Kissing—Intelligent children—Absence of religious notions—Differences of language—Ancient gold workings—Worship of Isis—Mosaic Law—Small-pox—Inoculation—Native vanity—Inferior iron-work—Carved snuff-boxes—Fire-sticks—Principal food—Produce—Curious calabashes—Disgusting reports—Chiconga's return visit—A chief's assegai—A demand for fire-water—A Woman's Rights argument—The royal baby—An endless visit—Jonosso to the rescue—The Queen retires.

TAKING advantage of one of the rare occasions when we had a free day, we paid a visit to Chiconga, M'Tassa's favourite daughter. The chieftainess inhabited a kraal five miles distant from New Umtali. It was said to be a very picturesque spot, and well worth a visit. Accompanied by Mr. Walter Sutton, and attended by two native boys, we therefore set out one morning soon after six o'clock. We were on foot; the boys carrying beads and limbo, as we wished to trade for a cow.

Our path led us for some distance along the high road to Fort Salisbury, a picturesque track, winding between thickly-wooded hills. Here and there it struck over the open veldt, skirting the strange granite kopjes, which form an important feature in Mashonaland landscape. These piles of colossal boulders, springing abruptly from a tableland of veldt, look as if they had been built up by giants. Trees clothe the summit of these kopjes, and wild beasts lurk in the caves formed by their overhanging rocks.

On the topmost pinnacle of the largest of them, Chiconga and her people had built their village. From this eminence the approach of an enemy could be distinguished whilst he was yet miles away. Nor was the precaution a vain one. The Mashonas are a nation of rabbits scared by a gesture, peaceful and indolent. But Gungunyama, the great Gazaland chief, has, more than once, sent his warriors to raid in Manica. We were told that it had often happened that three or four of his men entered a kraal, massacred a hundred Mashonas, and carried off women and cattle, without encountering an attempt at resistance. Hence the Mashonas build their villages in the most inaccessible places.

We found Chiconga's kraal very difficult to reach. The path was so steep as to be almost perpendicular. Only one person could advance at a time, and without the aid of our surefooted boys we should never have reached the summit. Hot and breathless, we were glad to rest on a grassy plateau outside the high stockade which enclosed the kraal.

Here a number of natives were lying under the shadow of a tree. Some were binding together the split reeds of which native mats are made. Others were playing a game that seemed nearly related to draughts. The men were made of bits of wood; the board had been roughly mapped out on the rock with the "chipanga," or knife, which all natives carry. One and all professed great surprise at our appearance, though of course we knew they had seen our approach more than an hour before, and had probably watched with amusement our struggles up the steep sides of the kopje. When we asked for admittance to the kraal one of the natives pushed aside a heavy door swinging between two rocks, and invited us to enter. The door was made of wood, black with age, and was evidently half of the trunk of an enormous tree, of a species no longer existing in the country. In order to follow our guide we had to bend nearly double, the entrance was so low; and in this undignified position we made our entry to the village.

This consisted of a group of wretched huts, badly built and thatched. In the midst of these were several circular earth-works—not unlike colossal acorn-cups. These were thatched more carefully. We were told that they were the granaries of the community. The plateau on which the huts were built was kept fairly clean. Pigeons fluttered among the dwellings. Imp-like children darted in and out of the rocks.

The view from this spot was splendid. Unrolled at our feet, like a huge map, the plain stretched away for leagues, mingling at length with the distant hills that fringed the horizon. We should have liked to admire it for many moments, but the headman, or induna, now appeared, and requested us to go to the "council hut." So, creeping through a low door, we seated ourselves on clean mats which had been spread out for us. Our natives squatted outside.

After we had waited for some time, a loud clapping of hands was heard, and Chiconga made her appearance, followed by fifty or sixty men. She entered the hut, and squatted on a mat opposite to us. As soon as she was seated, she began to sway backwards and forwards, and clap her hands. This is a greeting expressive of welcome and respect. We wondered whether we too ought to clap, and I put the question in Portuguese to our boy. He answered, "No," and entered the hut, and after clapping and bobbing for a long time, stood up and made a speech. He informed Chiconga that we were great chieftainesses and witch-women. The white man came to us sick, and we healed him. The country belonged to us; the white men were our servants. We spoke, and they made thunder and lightning! Whenever he paused, the "warriors," who crouched behind Chiconga—and who, by the way, could not have said Boh! to a goose—clapped loudly.

Chiconga then declared that we were welcome. She was small, slight, very ugly, and not unlike an ill-nourished monkey. A piece of very dirty blue limbo was wound round her. We thought her very much less queen-like than the Maquaniqua who had come to see us at Sabi Ophir. But she was a gentle savage, not without mother-wit. The Bishop relates in his Journal, that, having paid her a visit, he asked if she would like to learn his religion. After a moment's silence, she answered: "If you do not proceed on your way, it will be dark before you reach the next village." Truly a woman, savage or civilized, is rarely at a loss for an answer!

Our boys now unpacked the trading stuff, and, first offering the chieftainess a present of a gaily-striped blanket, we proceeded to trade for a cow, fowls, mealies, and other things we wanted. Each family had something to sell, pumpkins, white beans, or eggs.

They were very particular about the colour and size of the beads they accepted. Fashion is as autocratic in a native kraal as in the big village by the Thames. Blue and white beads had been the rage six months before; now no one could possibly wear anything but red ones. They were very particular too about the limbo they liked. Far from delighting in gaudy and grotesque patterns, they only approved of plain colours—dark blue or crimson. They preferred white to anything. Chiconga took £2 and four blankets for a very pretty cow. She presented us with a pair of pigeons in return for the blanket we had offered on arriving.

It amused us to see the respect with which her followers treated her. Whenever she spoke, they clapped. Once she went to the door, and spat outside; they all clapped solemnly! Meanwhile no other woman dared approach the "council hut."

They seemed a simple, harmless people; yet bursts of ferocity were not uncommon among them.

A blind man, who used to wander about Manica, playing on a native piano, from which he extracted sounds not unlike those produced by a Jew's harp, was an example of this. He was an unusually good-looking man, in spite of his sightless eyes, and had married some relation of the chief M'Tassa. He had several wives, but the savour of forbidden fruit is relished in Manica as well as in Paris, and in an evil hour for him it was discovered that he had been paying court to a neighbour's wife. Consulting together, his "lawful wives" seized him one night; tied him to a tree; and, whilst one held a torch, another tore his eyes out with a cow horn. The next day they drove him from the kraal, and since then he had wandered from place to place—a homeless man.

Since our return home, many people have asked us whether kissing is a natural expression of affection, or a product of civilisation. Decidedly the latter; and I have never seen any native show signs of strong affection for either mothers or children. The latter are very quick and intelligent, capable of learning almost anything that it may occur to one to teach. But, as they grow up, they seem to become dull. The savage's intelligence, unlike that of a white man, ceases to develope at a very early age. In working with natives it is necessary to be very careful never to alter the routine they have been taught. If a boy has been accustomed to wash cups before plates, and you reverse the order, he will spend the day in a state of bewilderment. We took a great deal of trouble to find out what notions of religion the Mashonas possessed. It was, however, impossible to discover that they believed in anything. Asked if they believed in a life after death, they usually shrieked with laughter at such an idea. "An ox dies, you buy another. A man dies, you cannot replace him. That is the only difference." We could never get a more satisfactory answer, and Mr. Selous told us that he had had the same experience. We heard, however, that at one or two kraals the natives were beginning to believe that their chiefs had spirits, which, after death, animated lions or serpents, and often haunted the village.

Unlike the Matabele or the Zulu, the Mashonas did not appear to form one tribe. The different groups of kraals seemed to have little to do with each other. Indeed two natives, living but a few miles from each other, often spoke quite a different dialect. For instance, one would call a door "lima," —another "rufa." Some made continual clicking sounds, from others you never heard a click at all. Though nominally king of Manica, M'Tassa had little authority outside his own kraal, and even within its limits it was often disputed.

Some authorities are of opinion that the Mashonas were the descendants of Egyptian slaves, brought to Manica in gangs to work the gold. The whole country is riddled with old workings. Some of the mountains are honey-combed with drives and tunnels. The fact that the natives dance to the new moon, without appearing to know why, is said to be a trace of the worship of Isis. That a childless widow marries her brother-in-law, and that any children she may have rank as those of her dead husband, is considered to be a trace of the law of Moses.

One and all inoculate for small-pox, making three punctures above the elbow. Questioned as to the origin of this practice, they told us that, "more moons ago than there were men on earth," a "great chief" had taught them to do it. These native kraals are said to be the original homes of small-pox, and are rarely free from it. As a rule the disease takes a mild form, but when we were in Manica, many hundreds were said to have died from it. Certainly inoculation had failed to check the spread of the malady. Yet the various doctors, who examined the boys' arms, appeared to think the operation had been well, and even very neatly, performed.

In general the Mashona is undersized and thin. Many of them, however, though small, were beautifully made. They were all muscle, hard as steel, with small bones and skins of exceeding fineness and beauty. Many a lady might envy the smallness of their hands, the slenderness of their wrists and ankles. Now and then one came across a native so purely Egyptian in type, so melancholy and impassive, that he might have been a Pharaoh working out his Karma—a slave among slaves.

Natives spend an immense time adorning themselves. Many of them plait their wool into hundreds of little tails, which stick up all over their heads. Beads, buttons, and bits of brass wire are often woven into these tails. Some weave their hair into a sort of bird's nest; others into a castellated structure, which must take years to perfect. They adorn themselves with bead necklaces and tiger-cat skins. They are not keen hunters, being too timid to chase either lions or leopards.

Their pottery consists only of large round earthenware pots, coarsely made, which serve to keep water cold on the hottest day. The natives also cook in them. Their iron work for assegai blades or arrow-heads is very poor indeed. The arrow-heads in especial are remarkably rude, and far inferior to those made in other parts of Africa. But they carve beautiful little snuff-boxes, and curious wooden head-rests to sleep upon.

The brass work too on some of their knives was very well done. They still use the fire-sticks for producing fire, though such kraals as are in touch with the white men have learnt to appreciate Bryant and May. They live principally on "Kaffir corn," as it is called. This grain grows on stalks, not unlike mealie-stalks, which reach the height of ten or eleven feet. It is dark, like linseed, when cooked, and has a heavy, sweetish taste. We used it with great success for poultices.

The natives also grow rice, tobacco, sweet potatoes, sugar-cane in small quantities, and pumpkins. Out of gourds they make curious drinking vessels. Whilst the gourd is still growing they tie thongs of bark tightly round it in different places, thus forcing the fruit to grow in strange, quaint shapes. The most usual arrangement is that of a long straight handle, with a cup-like bowl at one end. When the fruit is ripe the natives carefully scoop out the interior, and dry the rind in the sun. These "calabashes" are very useful. The native stands on a rock, or on a bank, and by means of his long-handled "calabash" scoops up the river water without wetting himself. Except when engaged in swimming and diving, the Mashona has a horror of getting wet. His dread of rain is strange, considering that he has no clothes to spoil.

Though these natives live chiefly on vegetable diet, they are very fond of meat. If a cow dies anywhere on the veldt, they troop to it, disputing its carcase with the vultures. A number of natives will encamp round the spoil, and not move till the last bone has been picked clean. Decomposition has no terror for them. They enjoy a smell which sickens the very jackals.

With all their faults, we could not help getting fond of our boys; they were invariably cheerful, and they moved so noiselessly. We always found the raw native to be strictly honest.

The day after we had visited Chiconga's kraal, she sent us a messenger bearing an assegai entirely made of iron. These spears being only used by chiefs, it is considered an honour to receive one. Chiconga was not far behind her messenger. She arrived with an escort of sixty or seventy people—old and young men, and boys of all ages. One of these last carried her baby.

Being made welcome, and requested to enter our hut, the "Queen" seated herself on a box, while her husbands sat on the ground beside her. We offered her a present of limbo and beads, then, sending for coffee, handed her a cup. This she did not like the look of. Therefore, in spite of his reluctance, one of her husbands had to taste it first. He disapproved emphatically, spitting it out behind the box on which his wife was seated. Chiconga then declined the coffee, suggesting that she understood, and liked, whisky better. We told her that "firewater" was the drink of men, not of women, but we could not make her see the force of the argument. If white men liked it and drank it, why should not white women do so? What was good for men, was good for women too, at least for chieftainesses! This Woman's Rights argument finding voice in a country where women are mere beasts of burden, amused us greatly. We compromised the question. We had received a present of port wine, and now offered her some. This beverage met with her approval. But, finding her prepared to drink mugsfull of it there and then, we were forced to violate the laws of hospitality, and have the bottle carried away.

A tin of lump sugar had been sent to us a few days before. This sugar delighted Chiconga, who ate quantities of it, and begged for some to take away—a request which we of course acceded to. Every now and then the baby, which had remained outside with all the other followers, set up a shrill cry—then its mother would run out and feed it. Remembering that in lying-in-hospitals there is a stringent rule that babies must be fed regularly, at stated intervals, I was interested to note that the savage infant is allowed to suck as often as it likes, and thrives exceedingly on these irregular repasts. A white baby, fenced in by rules and regulations, smothered in a bundle of senseless clothes, is an unhappy little atom compared to his black brother.

Before long we began to wonder when Chiconga meant to go. There seemed no near prospect of getting rid of her. At length a happy thought occurred to us. We had got a small block of incense, such as the Malays use during their ceremonies. We told Jonosso to light some, and fumigate the hut. When he had done so, he gravely informed Chiconga that farewells ought to follow incense burning. Upon which she arose, offered us her hand *à l'Anglaise*, and departed with all her train.

CHAPTER X

A tale of horror—" Smelling out witches "—Maronka—His prisoner—An expedition to rescue him—The encampment—Lions—Native carried off—Half devoured—Horses attacked—Night of terror—A plucky terrier—The dead lioness—Maronka submits—Mr. Carden—Home again—Another lion story—Vogler—Besieged by lions—A terrible situation—No water—Rescued—Too late—Vogler's death—More lions—Siege of Umtali—Warlike funeral—Night alarm—A reign of terror—Township attacked—Tracked to his lair—The dead monarch—Lying in state—At peace once more.

Two or three people—amongst them Mr. Bent—having spent three months in Mashonaland, assert that lions do not exist there. Such is not our experience, as the following pages will show.

One morning a native entered the camp, bringing a tale of horror to the Magistrate's ear. A chief called Maronka, whose kraal was about forty miles distant, had seized his family and boiled them alive. He and his brother had escaped, but the latter had been recaptured, and he himself pursued as he fled to Umtali to ask the protection of the White Chief.

Maronka and his people had emerged from the state of belief in nothing, and were passing through the barbarous superstitious stage. They believed that, after death, the souls of their chiefs passed into the bodies of lions, though still holding that the generality of the tribe were soulless. They had powerful witch-doctors, and "smelt-out" witches, much in the manner described in Rider Haggard's novels.

The family of the native who had escaped to our camp had been "smelt out," and, if his brother were not rescued, he would be condemned to some horrible death.

The Magistrate immediately sent out police to demand the release of the prisoner. Receiving no satisfactory answer, he set out with his men to force the chief to yield.

The first night's camp was undisturbed;

and, next day, the white men reached the foot of the kopje on the top of which Maronka's kraal was perched. The night was moonless, the darkness intense. Having collected a quantity of wood, two circles of fires were lit. In the outer circle were the natives and some of the white men; in the inner circle the rest of the police and the horses.

Towards one o'clock in the morning the Magistrate went round to see that the fires were being kept up, and the watchmen at their posts. Before turning in he paused to replenish a fire in the outer circle, near which he himself was sleeping. The flames leapt up, shedding a ruddy glare which emphasised the surrounding darkness. One or two natives were sleeping by the fire. As the Magistrate turned away, a monstrous dark shape bounded over the flames, seized a native, and vanished with him as noiselessly as it had appeared.

The alarm was given, and in an instant the encampment was on foot. The native who had been carried away did not lose consciousness or presence of mind. "This way," he kept shouting. "Maïwé! oh, maïwé!"—the native cry of anguish or of terror. "The lion, the lion! he is eating my shoulder. Oh, my head! This way—this way! Quickly, white man!"

Several shots were fired in the direction of the cries; and then, seizing flaming logs, a number of men rushed out into the darkness and long grass, firing as they went. Suddenly the light of the torch revealed a horrible sight. A large lioness was lying on the unfortunate native, crunching up his shoulder. Again they fired, and, with a sullen roar, the great beast sprang into the grass and disappeared. Hurriedly they bore her victim back to the fires. Three minutes had scarcely elapsed since the lioness had leaped the fire in search of prey, but the poor native was in a pitiable condition. The whole of one shoulder and arm was a mass of shapeless, bloody pulp, and his scalp was torn from his head. He lived till morning, not appearing to suffer greatly, but, as the first rays of sunlight fell on his face, he uttered a cry and expired.

Meanwhile a shout from the natives, who had swarmed up trees, drew attention to the horses. A lion bounded in amongst them, undeterred by noise or fires. The horses broke loose, and stampeded. Growls, snarls, a cry in the darkness, the sound of galloping horses, the ravings of the dying native, filled the remaining hours of the night with terror. It was indeed a relief to all when the sudden tropical day dawned at last. Action was now possible. Anything was better than sitting there in the darkness, waiting for what might happen.

The first thing to do was to track and slay the lioness, and recover the horses—or such among them as were still alive. A plucky terrier called "Syndicate," who afterwards became our dog, set the party on the track of the lioness, actually putting her up like a partridge. He would have fallen a victim to his temerity, had not a timely shot disposed of the great cat. She had been severely wounded the night before, which accounted for her remaining so close to the encampment. When the carcase was opened, it was found that she must have been many days without food. Much to their surprise and satisfaction, the police recovered all the horses. One or two were badly mauled, nearly all were scratched, but none of them died. It was conjectured that the other lions were large cubs. Had they been full grown, the horses would not have got off so easily.

A messenger was now sent up to Maronka, informing him that if the prisoner were not delivered up within a certain time, the white men would seize his kraal and drive him out. After a very short palaver, Maronka yielded, sending back the prisoner, also a present of goats and fowls, to propitiate the wrath of the whites.

The chief and his people believed that the lions which had attacked the encampment were animated by the souls of former chiefs seeking to defend the kraal. Since the whites had overcome the great Spirits, the resistance of mere mortals would be absurd. Maronka never gave any further trouble. One of the officers of the police, Mr. Carden, who is said to have shown unusual pluck during this night of horror, wrote a capital description of this episode to his people. It appeared in the *Field*, and excited much interest.

News travels with incredible swiftness in Africa, losing nothing on the way. Long before the police returned, we heard vague and alarming accounts of lions, of men torn to pieces, and of horses killed. It may be imagined, therefore, how glad we were to see the expedition return safe and sound. More especially were we glad to welcome back Mr. Carden, who was one of our best friends. His hut, in the officers' quarters of the camp, was near our compound, and whenever we were in any difficulty—which was often— "Send for Mr. Carden," was the cry! Such a nice boy! full of fun, and steady as old Time. The type of a young English gentleman, whose people for generations had "feared God and honoured the king." He it was who told us another lion tale,—almost more terrible than the Maronka affair.

A prospector named Vogler, camped somewhere between Beira and Umtali, was searching for a reef supposed to be lying in that direction. One day some natives came to his camp, telling him that two white men were "besieged by lions" a hundred miles away, and that both were dead or dying. Vogler wasted no time, he knew that white men were encamped at the place indicated by the natives, and found that the latter, questioned individually, told a consistent tale. Taking with him a guide and a few boys to carry provisions, he walked the hundred miles in less than two days and a half.

In front of the solitary hut, built at some distance from water, lay the bones of a lion; several more had their lair in the bushes close by, according to the natives. With some difficulty Vogler obtained admission to the hut. There he found two white men in an indescribable condition. One man was lying on a rude stretcher apparently unconscious; the other was up and about, but looked a ghastly object. An intolerable smell poisoned the atmosphere. Having attended to the first wants of these two miserable men, Vogler asked what had happened. The man who was still conscious told him.

His comrade, he said, had caught the fever, was very ill, and too weak to move. The natives had deserted, as they so often do in face of sickness. One night, hearing a noise round the hut, he thought the boys might have returned—perhaps with evil intentions. Taking his rifle, he threw open the door. It was a bright moonlight night. Straight in front of him, at a distance of about twenty paces, stood a large lion; he fired, and killed it. As he lowered his gun, the lioness, which he had not perceived, stole noiselessly round the hut, seized his right hand, and literally tore it off. The man had presence of mind enough to dart back into the hut, and bang the door. It was a frail protection, being made of reeds; but in spite of the terrible wound he found strength enough to pile sacks of rice against it. His right arm was a ghastly stump, the broken bones sticking out through the bleeding flesh below the elbow. His hand was gone. Fearing that he would bleed to death, he melted a quantity of brown sugar and plunged the stump into it. It was, when Vogler saw it, still coated over with a hard mass of sugar.

He now no longer dared to leave the hut. He and his friend had provisions, but no water. Part of their store was composed of tins of salmon and sardines. They bored holes in the tins, and drank the oil, and the horrible fish liquid. In this manner they had lived for seven days! The man with fever had got gradually worse, and appeared likely to die, but he eventually recovered. Unfortunately, it was impossible to save the wounded man. The arm was gangrened and he died soon after Vogler's arrival. The latter himself told the story to Mr. Carden.

Not long after, Vogler also went " beyond the sunset." He ordered himself to be carried to the hospital, but died in his "machila" before reaching it. His death took place in one of the loveliest spots near Umtali. There the road dips into a "donga." On the one side the sunlit veldt spreads away; on the other a dense thicket casts a grateful shade over the road. At the time of year of which I am writing this thicket was ablaze with brilliant flowers—the blossoms of a sort of azalea. Every shade of red was here represented, from the palest faded rose to the most intense scarlet. Bright-coloured birds flitted through the branches. Butterflies, with wings of metallic lustre, floated over the flowers. A perpetual hum of insects suggested drowsy summer idleness; strange enervating perfumes steeped the senses in languor. It was surely a dreamy poetical place from whence to drift into the unknown. I am told, however, that this is quite a mistaken sentiment; that to die in a bed, in a shaded room, with hospital walls around you, instead of banks of flowers, is a more suitable ending—"more satisfactory to one's friends." It may be so. For my part

I envied Vogler's mode of passing away. "It is better to hear the lark sing than the mouse chepe," says the north-country proverb. I am sure it is full of wisdom, even though the listener's ears be dying ones.

The roar of a lion, once the most familiar of nightly sounds, had, so far, never been heard in New Umtali. A visit from the king of beasts was the last thing any one expected; it was, therefore, sure to be paid before long.

One day two men drove from Salisbury to Umtali, borrowing, for the purpose, Dr. Jameson's mule cart. One of these gentlemen was a Mr. Robert Williams, well known in Africa as a successful speculator and a right good fellow. He was no novice in African travel, and scarcely was his cart outspanned, than he asked if it was safe to leave the mules on the veldt for the night. Yes, was the universal answer. Between camp and township, oxen and donkeys roamed about all night; none of them had ever been lost.

Captain Heyman, of Masse-Kesse fame,

had returned to Umtali as Resident Magistrate and Civil Commissioner. The officials had hitherto succeeded each other like pictures in a magic-lantern, but Captain Heyman bade fair to be an exception to the rule. He had invited Mr. Williams to be his guest.

That night we were up nearly all night with a bad case. Dr. Johnston had been recalled home; his substitute had not arrived; it was a time of anxiety of which I propose to speak in another chapter. One of us crossing over to the hospital on the night in question, was startled by a terrible yell,—a prolonged agonising shriek. It reminded one of the legends of the Banshee.

As soon as the camp was astir, we sent to ask Mr. Carden if he had heard the noise, and knew what it was. His answer was a startling one. Lions had invaded the hitherto peaceful camp; a mule, a donkey, and an ox had been killed within a few yards of the hospital. Two more mules were killed in the bush close to the Police Camp. It was the shriek of a mule, which the lion had disembowelled, that we had heard. The other creatures had had their necks broken, and died instantaneously. A lion springs on an ox, passes a paw under his jaw, gives his head a twist, and his neck is broken. The whole operation takes place with such rapidity that the ox cannot attempt to save itself, and, after the first moment of terror, probably suffers nothing.

We heard no more of the lions for that day, but, after all the wild tales that floated about, it was impossible to cross the compound after dark without a thrill of terror. Our watch that night was a dismal one. Seated beside the dying man whose life was ebbing slowly away, we listened nervously to every sound, momentarily expecting some terrible catastrophe. Nothing happened, and at last morning dawned, and the terrors of the night seemed to vanish with the darkness. Our boys, however, informed us that the mules had again been attacked in the shelter in which they had been tied up, and had stampeded. One had fled away towards

Salisbury, the other had been killed far from the camp. The lions, then, were still at hand. They were, indeed, nearer than any one supposed. At nine o'clock we saw a commotion in the Police Camp. The men had seized their rifles, and were all hurrying in one direction.

It appeared that a native who herded the cattle suddenly saw a lion spring out of the grass, and give chase to the oxen. He very nearly caught one, springing at it and scratching it very severely. The natives' shouts scared the brute and raised the alarm in camp, the men turning out at once. Many shots were fired; the pursuit was a hot one, but unsuccessful, the long grass making it impossible to see more than a few feet ahead. However, the lions were supposed to have been driven off. Not a bit of it! That very afternoon they returned about four o'clock, and, in broad daylight, coolly chased the police horses across the commonage between the township and the camp. One of the horses had a very narrow escape.

That morning our patient died. His funeral, which took place the same afternoon, was a strange spectacle, most of the men being armed with rifles. The procession looked more like a war-like expedition than a funeral.

By this time our huts were furnished with solid doors, but the large window in our sleeping hut was simply a hole in the wall. We barricaded this with a big umbrella, hoping that the lion would object to its size and spikes. Mr. Carden brought us a revolver, and Captain Heyman had a lantern hung outside in a tree. A lion is said to object to a lantern, and perhaps he does. In any case, he did not try to enter our hut. Every one, however, was not so lucky.

Towards one in the morning we were roused by the most frightful yells that ever mortal lungs gave utterance to. We distinguished clearly the "Maïwé!" of the natives. A number of shots were fired in rapid succession, then all was silent.

In about half an hour the cries were repeated; more shots were fired; then came unbroken silence till morning. As soon as it was light we went to our boys' hut to find out what had happened, fully expecting to hear that some one had been carried off. It was a great relief to hear that no one had been injured. Captain Heyman's boys, however, who lived in a grass hut close to our compound, had had a narrow escape.

Alarmed by the nightly raids that had been made on the cattle, these natives kept a bright fire in their huts all night. One of them was making it up, when the whole party was roused by the well-known pig-like grunt of a hunting lion. Whilst they huddled together, the thatch wall was torn aside, and the head of a lion forced through the opening. His jaws were open; the huge cavity showed red in the firelight, which lit up his gleaming teeth and cruel yellow eyes. With one accord the boys burst into the wails and shrieks that had roused us and the police camp, thereby scaring off the lion. The night was of inky blackness. Nevertheless Captain Heyman, Mr. Williams, and Mr. Carden rushed out of their huts and fired their rifles—they could not see to aim at anything. Some one then appeared with a lantern, and the natives were convoyed to the mess hut, which was provided with a strong door. They declared that half an hour later the lion returned and tried to force his way through the door. At the first sound of the cries, the same men rushed out again and fired. The next morning the "spoor" showed that the lion must have passed close to Captain Heyman as he fired. It was a curious thing that just before the first alarm, Mr. Williams, who was sleeping in Captain Heyman's hut, should have declared that he heard a lion outside. Captain Heyman assured him that it was quite impossible. No lion, he said, would venture into the camp and wander among the huts. If it went anywhere, it would try and get into the stable. He had hardly finished speaking when the yells of his boys proved very convincingly that no one can calculate on what a wild beast will or will not do.

Every effort was now made to destroy the lions. The carcases of the mules were poisoned. Men sat up in the trees above them all night, on the chance of getting a shot. Mr. Carrick, the plucky postmaster, did this night after night, in all weathers, but in vain. The darkness was so dense that the shots which he fired in the direction from whence the sounds of crunching came, did not even frighten the lion. He merely dragged his mule a little further off, and went on with his supper. Nor did the poison seem to trouble him. The dispensary had none strong enough, or in sufficiently large quantities, to prove effectual.

For ten days there was a reign of terror in Umtali. The roads and streets of the township were covered with lion spoor. No one would venture out after dark. The natives took their assegais when they went to fetch water; most of the white men who had to go any distance took their revolvers or rifles. Hunting parties went out in different directions nearly every day, but were always unsuccessful. The lions on the contrary killed something every night. At last the climax came.

One night sounds of bellowing and trampling floated across to us from the township. Shots were fired, and evidently a great commotion was going on. It appeared that the lions had forced their way into a cattle kraal built behind one of the houses. The terrified cattle stampeded, their assailants chasing them through the streets. The noise was tremendous. Frightened faces appeared at windows, and rifles were discharged, but the lions paid no attention. They killed two oxen—one in the High Street, one near the oven of our friend the baker—besides badly mauling several others. This state of things could no longer be borne. One of the townsfolk, a good shot and clever hunter, took some natives with him, and followed up the fresh "spoor," which led into the bush behind the township. After walking some hours, they entered a small open glade, and there before them stood lion and lioness. A shot killed the former, his mate escaping into the undergrowth.

The dead king was carried back in triumph to Umtali. We all went to see him. He lay stretched out on the grass, a group of the people he had so long held in awe standing around. He was a beautiful beast, just in his prime, measuring ten feet long from the tip of his nose to the end of his tail. His coat was soft and bright, and of a tawny colour—not unlike that of a mastiff—with black points. This colour is so like that of the sun-dried grass, that it can with difficulty be distinguished from it. Altogether we thought him much handsomer than the menagerie lion, which is apt to look out of proportion—the head enormous, and the hindquarters falling away.

After the death of her mate, the lioness took her cubs away from Umtali, and wandered off towards the coast. She met her death in a mountain defile, called Christmas Pass—the very spot where Mr. Teal had been devoured by a lion more than a year before.

After these days of unpleasant excitement Umtali relapsed into its usual somewhat monotonous routine, nor did any such terrible visitants reappear during the remainder of our stay there.

CHAPTER XI

A luxury—Mr. Seymour-Fort—An eccentric drive—A luncheon party—China *versus* tin—Ill-behaved guests—Moonlight—Our carriage and pair—" Pills and Powders "—Their friendship with our monkey—Warned of a snake—An execution—Dr. Johnston departs—No doctor—A patient from Masse-Kesse—Clark and Paget—Amusing notes—The doctor at last—A *cause célèbre*—Troublesome results—What's in a name?—Gold finds—The gold fever—Wonderful reefs—The Queen of Sheba's kingdom.

NEARLY a year after our arrival at Umtali, just when climate and work were beginning to tell on us, we were able to indulge in a great luxury; thanks to the intervention of Mr. Seymour-Fort. This gentleman had renounced political life, and had come up to Mashonaland with some of the Directors of the British South Africa Company. He was, at the time of which I write, managing large mining interests. We had had the good fortune to see a great deal of him, and he ranks as the most valued friend we made in Africa.

Mr. Seymour-Fort had made the acquaintance of a miner, who possessed a small hand-cart—a very light vehicle, in fact, a mere box on wheels. He had lengthened the düselboom and harnessed two donkeys to it, the result being a convenient little trap.

Our first drive in this eccentric vehicle was most amusing. Scarcely had we started, the donkeys tearing madly down a steep donga, when the seat fell out, landing us at the bottom of the cart. I was driving Sister Aimée; Mr. Fort running alongside; a black boy trotting behind. Mr. Algernon Caulfield met us at the bottom of the donga, just in time to extricate us. The reins, which were made of rope, were much too long, and had tied us up in a complicated knot. The seat having been recovered and replaced, we made another start. But the donkeys suddenly refused to go on. Mr. Caulfield pushed, Mr. Fort pulled, we all shrieked encouragement in chorus, but nothing moved the donkeys. Suddenly, during a pause in our efforts, they rushed on again, nearly upsetting the seat a second time.

Finally, however, we arrived at Mr. Fort's camp safe and sound. Here a surprise awaited us in the shape of a real luncheon, neatly laid on a real tablecloth. Actually there were china cups! No one who has not been obliged to drink tea out of tin mugs can realise the pleasure of drinking it out of china. These cups eventually found their way to the hospital. We could not understand having two forks in the course of a meal, and were disposed to cling desperately to those we had used. Mr. Seymour-Fort declared that he had never entertained such ill-behaved people. We screamed at the appearance of a *bonâ-fide* teapot, and went into positive rapture when a salad was served.

After luncheon we decided on walking home through the valley, as it was rather dull having to return by the same road. Abandoning the "carriage," we descended the steep hill, on the top of which Mr. Fort's camp was pitched, and walked through the tall grass and rich vegetation of the narrow valley below, where groups of palms, sheltered by hills from the violent winds that sweep over the plain, wave their graceful branches on the banks of sleepy streams.

It was hot, but not unpleasantly so. By and by the sun sank in the west, and we finished our walk by moonlight. The fairy-like beauty of tropical moonlight can only be felt; it cannot be described. It seemed a crime to turn one's back on a scene of such beauty, and go prosaically to bed. But prose eventually carries the day in all such situations—worse luck! The next day a bad case was brought to the hospital. We had done well to take advantage at once of a day's freedom.

This expedition had been so successful, that Mr. Fort suggested that we should buy the donkey-cart. He would exchange a pair of excellent donkeys, "accustomed to harness," for two which the Bishop had given us. We accepted the offer with joy. A bargain was soon struck with the digger who owned the cart, and we became possessed of a " carriage and pair"! This equipage was a great resource. When patients were convalescent and up, we could harness the "thoroughbreds" and escape for an hour. The combination of fresh air without exertion, and an entire change of scene, though only attainable for so short a time, did us a world of good. When we got back to the wards we could be cheery without an effort, and had generally something to tell our patients about our driving adventures.

It was rarely that our drives were quite uneventful. The donkeys — sweet beasts, which we christened " Pills and Powders"— had mouths like cast-iron, and nearly pulled my arms off. If they determined to abandon the road and tear madly over the veldt, no earthly force could stop them. The cart was so light that I could pull it myself, and it merely served to urge the donkeys on by clattering at their heels. Later on I got them in hand, and they were much better behaved.

Some one else was as delighted with our new acquisition as we were. This was Eric, our little blue monkey. No one ever had such a charming monkey before or since—so clean, so full of fun, and so affectionate. It was a sight to see him sitting on "Pills's" big, shaggy head, examining his long ears with great interest. Eric had an inquiring mind, and evidently wanted to know the reason of everything. He used to sit on the calves' backs as they were lying down asleep, pull their eyelids open and peep inside. They never seemed to mind a bit. He was a sort of sentinel too, giving notice of any stranger's approach. One day, being chained to a long pole in front of our sleeping-hut, he made an awful noise, shrieking, chattering, springing up and down, staring all the time into our hut. We picked him up, tried to pacify him, and brought him milk, but all in vain. Sister Aimée going presently into the hut to fetch something saw the cause of the disturbance. A large snake was gliding about the place, and, at her approach, it darted into my blankets. We summoned all the natives, who killed the reptile with their assegais.

It was lucky for us that we were both so fond of animals, for our life was, as a rule, very monotonous. For one day off, which we enjoyed immensely, we were weeks without the slightest break in the routine of cooking, nursing—nursing, cooking. No one with merely a professional interest in the work could have endured the life. The cases were nearly all of fever. Many were very bad, and had serious complications; we lost about ten per cent. But there was, of course, none of the life and variety of London hospital work. We had a coolie cook during the last rainy season we spent in Mashonaland. This was a very great help. We were both getting rather run down, and could not have gone on without one.

We had a curious experience at the beginning of these rains. Dr. Johnston was recalled to England. Mr. Caulfield, who was acting as dispenser, went with him. The doctor had been very good to us, and we regretted his departure deeply. A substitute had been appointed, but had not arrived. The patients in hospital were convalescent; we discharged them in a few days, hoping they would not be replaced till the new doctor arrived. This was a vain hope. Two days later a procession wound its way across the plain, appearing to come from Masse-Kesse. First walked a native carrying a note stuck in a split reed. He held the bamboo in front of him, like a candle-bearer in a procession, and every now and then the white note caught the rays of the sun. Then followed a "machila," that is, a sort of canvas hammock slung on a long pole, which two or four natives carry on their shoulders. Out of the hammock hung a limp-looking leg. We made out all this with our field-glasses. Two boys walked behind the "machila," but they carried no luggage on their heads—an ominous sign.

A mere traveller would certainly have stores and blankets. As we expected, the bearers made straight for the hospital, recognisable by its Red Cross flag. Was this indeed a terrible accident such as we had often talked of? We hoped against hope, and went down to the gate to receive the sick man.

The machila contained a young Englishman, who had been sent over from Masse-Kesse, a distance of about eighteen or twenty miles. Though this place is a very fever nest, the Mozambique Company had unfortunately no doctor there. Several sick were brought over to us from that place. Our new patient had remittent fever badly, and a twenty-mile journey in a broiling sun had not improved his condition. We had great trouble and anxiety about him. Before coming to us he had tried every sort of quack medicine, taking everything recommended by anybody, and swallowing all the remedies one after the other. We were very glad indeed to see him turn the corner.

There were a good many slight cases of

fever in the district, and we enjoyed driving the donkeys on what we called "our rounds." I called myself "Paget" and Sister Aimée "Andrew Clark." We were extremely professional on these visits, and were complimented on our excellent "bedside manner."

It was a time of anxiety of course; yet amusing things happened.

One day, for instance, a distant farmer sent us a note marked urgent, and thus conceived: "The Sisters are requested to send six strong sleeping-draughts at once by bearer. Writer has had fever—very weak—can't sleep." Sister Aimée explained that the administration of six strong sleeping-draughts would probably be followed by an inquest; and we sent him a mild one, which, we afterwards heard, answered very well. Another man wanted a dose of what he called "Hydrag: Perchlor: powder." This is a strong poison, being in other words corrosive sublimate. He meant calomel, but wished to impress us with his professional knowledge of medical terms. Another poor man was brought over from Masse-Kesse in a hopeless state. He lingered for a few days, and died in the midst of the lion scare described in a former chapter.

Soon after, the new district surgeon arrived. His boys had deserted him on the veldt. He had been days without food, and in a raging fever. He was still very ill, and had to spend a fortnight in hospital.

Umtali was, not long after, agitated by a *cause célèbre*.

In a moment of folly and impecuniosity one of the settlers paid his boys with gilded shillings, instead of with sovereigns. These coins, of the Jubilee type, were, when gilded, very like sovereigns, excepting for their weight. Some one, it was never known who, had brought them into the country for no good purpose. A native who had received several of these false coins, happened to tramp up to Salisbury, and to go shopping. Of course at the very first store he entered the fraud was detected.

An inquiry being instituted, a number of

other natives who had been similarly deceived appeared to give evidence. Their former master was arrested. Umtali was in a ferment. Public opinion was divided. Many declared it was "jolly sharp" of the delinquent. A shilling, they averred, was quite enough for a native—much too good for him, in fact.

The court-house was packed on the day of the trial. The white man being found guilty, great curiosity was evinced as to what his sentence would be. Would he have hard labour, or a fine? Betting ran high. Finally he was condemned to pay a fine of £50. No sooner was his condemnation made known than he became a sort of hero. Nothing was heard but "poor fellow—what hard lines!" Trusting that popular sympathy would take a substantial form, the prisoner declared that he could not pay. But the arm of the law was extended, and bore him off to gaol. After twenty-four hours of reflection in this retreat, the money was paid and he was released. For a long time after, no native would accept a sovereign, unless it had St. George and the Dragon on it. As it was difficult to obtain any gold at all, it may be imagined what trouble this reasonable prejudice gave to the whole community.

Umtali had been very steady for some time,—abnormally steady, some people said. A slight and rather amusing incident swung the pendulum back in the direction of former days.

A prospector arrived whose name was Mr. George Dam. Naturally enough he strolled into a bar, and asked for a drink. "And what is your name?" said one of the men standing by. "Dam," was the answer. "D—— yourself," was the immediate retort, "what is your name?"—"Dam, I tell you," cried the stranger. Unholy adjectives flew round. "What is his name?"—"Won't he give his name?"—"What is your name?" roared the whole assembly. "Dam," shrieked the prospector for the third time. This was more than could be endured, and a free fight ensued. I do not know which party was victorious; certain it is, that there were a great many black eyes walking about the next day, and it was some time before the town settled down again.

A great find of gold was made close to the township. The quartz was like white sugar, and was largely scattered with lumps as big as a pin's head, and flakes of visible gold. There were long yellow veins of gold, running through almost every specimen of quartz. At first it was supposed that the reef would become less rich as the shaft was sunk deeper. Instead of this it became richer and richer. The ferment and agitation of the community may be imagined. Every one rushed about in every direction, looking for the continuation of the reef; but I do not think any one found it.

People stumble on rich finds in unexpected places, which had been pronounced barren of metal a few weeks before. I myself have seen a piece of quartzite, which an expert had declared to be mere dirt that could not possibly carry gold, pan with extraordinary richness. It is this uncertainty which lends a special fascination to gold prospecting. The men with the most technical knowledge are not, therefore, the most successful.

We of course knew only by hearsay of the gold finds. But every one told us that the goldfields of Manica were extraordinarily good. This country is said to be the ancient land of Ophir where the Queen of Sheba reigned, and whence she sent gold, myrrh, and spices, to the Wise King. However, this, of course, is pure conjecture.

CHAPTER XII

The hospital empty at last—An expedition proposed—We trek to the Odzani—A picnic—Our camp by the "Slippery Drift"—The march to M'Tassa's kraal—A wearisome delay—The King appears—A noisy palaver—Offering a present—Kaffir beer—The King is photographed—Bushman drawings—Return home—Cattle stealing—A warlike expedition—The "Artillery" borrow our donkey-harness—An awful old woman—Return of the expedition—News of the Bishop's return—Nurses to relieve us—The Beira Railway—The Jesuit Mission—Splendid organisation.

It was in September 1892 that the hospital was first empty for a few days. It underwent a thorough renovating; the mud walls being re-dâghered, and the mats that covered them carbolised, where it was not possible to renew them. Everything being in apple-pie order, and the health of the country being good, Dr. Johnston, then on the eve of his departure for England, proposed that we should accompany him and the Civil Commissioner to M'Tassa's kraal.

This Chief was very rarely seen by any one. His large leisure was almost entirely employed in conjugating the verb to drink. More than once the Company's officials had gone over to his mountain lair, and had been obliged to return without having been received by him. On this occasion, however, he was almost sure to appear, since the annual present of £100, which the Company gives him, was to be presented.

We, of course, jumped at the idea, and proposed driving "Pills and Powders" as far as practicable, and then walking. This was, however, declared to be impossible. One of the camp Scotch-carts, which vehicle looks like a waggon cut in half, was put into requisition. A tent was deposited at the bottom, on the top of which rugs, blankets, etc., were piled. The men were to ride.

One fine morning, therefore, we climbed into our Scotch-cart, drawn by a span of eight oxen, and trekked gaily across the veldt. We halted for luncheon under a group of trees. There is something very enjoyable in these African picnics. The air is so pure, the sky so cloudless. There is no busy, hurrying, noisy town, in the background; immense solitudes surround one. With a certain sense of lotus-eating enjoyment, one abandons oneself to the influences of the hour. Leaning back in the shade of the cart, one lazily watches the natives lighting fires and boiling kettles; while, near at hand, the large-eyed oxen wander slowly along, crushing aromatic herbs beneath their tread as they feed. A thin column of blue smoke rises from the fires round which the boys sit, singing a monotonous chant, which harmonises with the surroundings as nothing else would. Then the water boils, tea is made, luncheon is ready. Surely bread and corned beef never could taste so good under any other circumstances! Such is my impression of this picnic, and of many like it.

Luncheon being over we inspanned, and set off again, reaching the " Slippery Drift " at the Odzani river at half-past four in the afternoon. Here we were to halt for the night. It was a lovely river, rushing over a granite bed, swirling round great boulders, and gliding swiftly and sombrely between dark granite cliffs. A narrow line of thick bush belted the river on either side.

This ford had received the name of "Slippery Drift," from the fact that the shallow water here covered flat granite rocks as smooth as glass. A horseman was never quite sure of reaching the other side without a ducking. Even on foot it was difficult to avoid slipping. When the rains had swollen the river it was very dangerous, for horse and rider would be swept away with resistless force if either made the slightest mistake. Often it was wholly impassable. In September it was, of course, quite shallow.

Our tent was pitched on the banks of this most picturesque river; and whilst we carried our towels behind a big rock and had a wash, tea was made ready. We sat on a semi-circle of big rocks, and sipped it slowly, wondering, as we did so, what sort of "five o'clock" the Queen of Sheba indulged in! A cheery little dinner in the tent followed, and then we strolled out in the moonlight, and sat on the rocks, watching the river and chattering, till Dr. Johnston declared he could no longer countenance such insanitary proceedings, and we must go to bed. Thereupon Sister Lucy and I retired to the tent, the men making themselves comfortable under the Scotch-cart, and the natives beside the fires.

The next morning we were up betimes, and after a hurried breakfast we got into the Scotch-cart, which the men pushed into the middle of the river. From there we were able to step on a rock, then on to another, and so safely to land. The men waded through. We then set out to walk to the King's village, a distance of about four miles. The path wound upwards along a mountain side, through a narrow defile. On either side huge rocks towered above us. Down below was a chaos of rocks and boulders.

The whole was intermixed with the scrubby bush which abounds in this part of Africa, though there seem to be no tall forest trees.

We all walked in the usual single file along a narrow native track. The whole of Africa is intersected by these paths, which are never straight, but curve from one side to another. We often asked why a native proceeds in this roundabout way, and one or two people told me that every one has a natural tendency to go more to the right than the left, and that instinct leads the native to correct this by taking a turn in the other direction. On the other hand, we constantly noticed that natives are incapable of making a straight line. They never put a mat down straight, nor can they build a straight wall, nor cut a straight furrow.

Our path wound higher and higher, and led to the foot of a steep cliff, up which we scrambled, arriving at a species of small plateau, with a precipice on one side and piles of rocks on the other. We could see no huts, though we were almost in the kraal.

The low beehives were built behind rocks or trees, and were so cleverly contrived as to be quite invisible to a raiding force. Indeed, we were told that an Impi of Gungunyama's men from Gazaland had declared this village to be quite impregnable, and had returned home, raiding as they went.

A messenger was sent on to inform M'Tassa of our arrival. Not a native was to be seen—though of course they had watched us encamp at the Odzani, and had probably followed us all the way to our present halting-place. After a few moments' delay we followed our messenger, and entered the outer kraal: the one in which the chief lives being a good deal higher up, and strongly stockaded. We were conducted by an Induna to a small hut, where fresh mats were put down for us; but, finding it likely that we should have to wait a long time, we had the mats taken outside, and, seated on them, watched the strange scene.

Every rock and boulder was covered with natives—men, women, and children. They looked like crowds of flies that had settled on the granite. They did not talk, but stared with all their eyes. I should think we must have waited an hour, and then sent a messenger to inquire whether M'Tassa meant to appear or not. The answer was that the Chief was coming. Meanwhile, he sent a huge pot of native beer, a rather nauseous compound made from Kaffir-corn. We waited another hour, and then it was proposed that we should stroll through the King's kraal. He would dislike this very much, and would probably put in an appearance.

We carried out this project, and no sooner were we inside the stockade, than an Induna hurried up to us, assuring us that M'Tassa would see us directly, if we would only go back to our mats. We did so, and in a few moments a great noise announced the approach of the Chief.

A picturesque procession came winding in and out through the crags and boulders, and descended slowly towards us. First ran a sort of herald, crying out, "Here comes M'Tassa!—Lord of the Sun and Moon!—The Dog that prowls by night!—The Eater up of white men!" and a great deal more foolishness. Then followed a number of men, the dignity of whose march was somewhat detracted from by the rags of dirty limbo in which many of them were draped. To these succeeded a man carrying a beautiful battle-axe, made of black polished wood, curiously inlaid with brass. After him came M'Tassa himself. He was a tall, stout man; draped in blue and white limbo, worn somewhat after the fashion of a toga; and with a blue and white cricketing cap on his head. His hair was woolly, but his features were rather fine. He walked well, and came forward with a decidedly dignified air, offering us his hand, which was slender and well-shaped, but extremely dirty. A mat was unrolled for the "King," and his men squatted round him. A good-sized tree threw its shadow over M'Tassa; a number of slender bamboos and young trees hid the rocks on this spot. No doubt the natives were accustomed to meet here for their dances and "palavers."

A most noisy "palaver" this was. Certain natives had run away from Mr. Selous, and were said to have stolen some meal. M'Tassa was requested to give them up. Our interpreter explained this to the head Induna, who in turn explained to his Chief. The latter kept up an admirable feint of never understanding anything that was said until his Induna explained it to him. He eyed us furtively, but always tried to pretend not to be looking at us if we caught his eye.

One party in the kraal were for giving up the boys; the other party was anti-white, and was headed by a ruffianly-looking person, who had combed out his wool until it had acquired quite a respectable length, and who was of an extremely ferocious appearance. He got up, and yelled and shouted, until M'Tassa shook his fists at him, and yelled louder still. Meanwhile we had been looking at the battle-axe with covetous eyes, and suddenly, forgetful of etiquette, exclaimed in Mashona, " M'Tassa! we want your battle-axe; will you trade?" A moment of shocked silence followed, then a hubbub, and then a good deal of laughing. M'Tassa good-naturedly caused his Induna to explain that he could not part with the weapon, because it always belonged to the Chief, and his son would have it after him.

To change the conversation, and divert the current of people's thoughts, the "present" was produced. Two rolls of limbo, one blue, one white, of about thirty yards each, were deposited in front of the Chief, and a hundred golden sovereigns were poured out on them. The king looked very slightly at it, and showed no pleasure. This is etiquette. After a few moments, M'Tassa condescended to explain through his head-man that he did not care for gold, but that he would accept limbo in place of it, since the white men were so anxious to make him presents.

This point being settled, Dr. Johnston

asked if he might photograph the chief and his people. He said he would take M'Tassa's likeness to England, and perhaps the "Great White Queen" would see it, and recognise what a great chief M'Tassa was. To everyone's surprise, permission was given, and a very characteristic and picturesque photograph was the result, though the King rather spoilt himself by pulling his "toga" up about his ears. The Chief now sent for a small pot of beer—his own special brew. We all tasted this, and found it really excellent. It was sweetened with honey, and was very different from the beer generally in use.

We were anxious to leave, having a good walk back to the Odzani, and being desirous of getting back to Umtali that evening. So Dr. Johnston put up his apparatus, and, evidently being looked upon as a great sorcerer by the natives, made his adieux to M'Tassa. We all hurried down the cliff, pausing at the bottom to search for a great rock, on which Mr. Selous had told us some interesting bushman drawings were to be seen—a proof that in some far distant time the bushmen lived in Mashonaland and Manica.

These bushmen are supposed to have been the original inhabitants of Africa. They are of low stature, their speech is made up of clicks, they have no settled dwellings, and they live altogether by hunting and fishing. They are, in fact, a very low order of savage. We could not find out, from any one who had been among them, whether the bushmen of these days show any talent for drawing. Their forefathers have left most beautiful and delicate specimens of their art, traced in yellow and red pigment on the rocks. The sketches reminded us of those executed by the cavemen — outlines of various kinds of buck, elephants, and other animals, dashed in with a boldness and directness which any modern animal painter might envy. No one could tell us of what the pigment was made. It seems wonderful that it should have withstood the weather, for who shall say how long! I am sorry to say that some white men of the "'Arry" species have thought it funny and clever to add to the collection. Another of these strange picture galleries exists near Fort Salisbury. We questioned the natives about them through the interpreter, but they could give no account of them. No one knew, they said; no one could count the moons since they were shaped. We thought them one of the most interesting sights we had seen in this strange land. It was, however, impossible to linger, and we hurried along to the waggon. The heat was great, and we were very glad indeed to see the Odzani glittering in the sun. We had an uneventful trek home, reaching the hospital when the moon was high.

Some short time after this excursion, a neighbouring kraal excited the wrath of the white men, by stealing the Company's oxen. The head-man of the village refused to give up the culprits, or make any compensation. In consequence, an expedition was planned to punish the kraal. A good trek-ox is a very valuable animal up in Mashonaland, and if one village had found it possible to steal cattle with impunity, the others would soon have imitated the example. It was decided that the erring kraal must be thoroughly frightened, and then fined.

Accordingly a Maxim gun was to be taken with the expedition. But how was it to be got there? That was the question! There was no harness to be had; and finally, to our great amusement, the "Government" borrowed our donkey harness. It was enlarged to fit a couple of horses, and the artillery was ready for action. We watched the start with much interest. But alas! at about five hundred yards from the hospital, the Maxim had to cross a small ford, lying at the foot of a steep hill. Here the horses jibbed, plunged, and could not be induced to go a step farther. Men were sent back to the camp for a span of oxen to replace the horses, and the expedition proceeded on its way. Evil fate pursued it however. Torrents of rain fell night and day. The

Maxim could not be dragged anywhere near the kraal, and had to be abandoned for the moment on the veldt.

Meanwhile news of these preparations had been noised abroad. The offending natives fled from their village—a wretched group of huts—taking cattle and goods with them. The Company's forces were met by one awful old woman, who denounced them in an unintelligible dialect. No doubt it was just as well that no one understood her. Natives have a fine talent for abuse of all kinds, and we heard that the old lady sounded as if she was saying "swears." The police burnt an empty hut as an example, and carried off a goat and a few fowls. They kindly brought us some curiosities in the shape of fire-sticks, arrows, a native piano, and a few odds and ends. They would have enjoyed being attacked by an impi, but the old woman struck terror into their souls. The Maxim was extricated, and came home meekly after the expedition had returned to Umtali. On the whole, perhaps, it was not a very successful venture. Still the fact that "the white man's thunder" had gone out on the war path produced a certain effect. At any rate no more cases of cattle stealing occurred.

The end of our two years' engagement was now rapidly approaching, and we were looking forward with great satisfaction to returning to England. The hospital was no longer a forlorn shed, but very fairly comfortable; we had a cook, a herd of cows, very good huts, and we could feel that the nurses who would replace us would not have many hardships to endure.

News that the Bishop who had gone to England in October, 1892, had actually left for Africa in February, 1893, was indeed welcome. For nearly a year there had been no clergyman in Mashonaland. We heard that Dr. Knight Bruce was bringing out clergy, nurses, and lay missionaries.

The railway from Fontesvilla, on the Pungwé, to Chimoio was progressing fairly well, considering the great difficulties caused by the formation of the country, the heavy rains, and the fever which inevitably rages wherever the virgin soil of a tropical country is dug up on a large scale. It was said that the Bishop thought of sending the nurses up by the Pungwé route, in order to set us free in April. We therefore telegraphed to Cape Town, offering to wait his convenience at Umtali. The rivers between Fontesvilla and Chimoio were swollen, and large tracts of the country were, for the time, converted into mere swamps. The railway works were at a standstill, in consequence, and every report that reached us from Beira spoke of danger and fever along the route. We felt therefore that it would be selfish on our part to be the cause in any way of involving two nurses fresh from England in such a risk. Of course it was not without a pang that we looked forward to waiting till June—or perhaps even July! But there was no help for it.

We heard from the Bishop soon after he arrived in Africa. He said he was very glad we had settled to wait till he could bring the nurses up by the long trek. He had had a most delightful spring-waggon made at Bristol, and he proposed sending the nurses up in this. They were from University College Hospital. He intended to engage one or two colonial nurses also. Dr. Knight Bruce went on to say many very flattering things about our work, and our usefulness to the Mission. We have kept all these letters; they are pleasant to read over in moments of depression. We very much wished we had been able to do more.

The Jesuit Mission at Fort Salisbury had made very rapid strides. We had arrived up country whilst the nuns were still at Tuli, and in 1893 seventeen religious sisters were in Mashonaland. They not only nursed the hospital at Fort Salisbury, but had opened a school there. At Victoria also, they had charge of the hospital.

The Rev. Father Kerr had a large industrial farm near Fort Salisbury, and we heard that a number of Jesuit lay-brothers were employed on it. In one of the Administrator's speeches, he said that he believed that the agricultural future of Mashonaland would be enormously indebted to this industrial farm. The Jesuits also worked very actively amongst the natives. They seemed to have no lack of money or workers, and to be most efficiently organised. Our efforts seemed very poor and small, when contrasted with the works they carried out on so large a scale. It may therefore be imagined how much we rejoiced over the long-looked-for return of the Bishop, and how glad we were to hear that he was largely supplied with funds, and would soon be able to place the Mission on a more satisfactory footing.

CHAPTER XIII

Illness—Visit from a leopard—Tedious convalescence—Again without a doctor—Arrival of the Bishop—New nurses on the way—Their arrival at Umtali—A split in the camp—A touching deputation—Farewell to Umtali—Fever *en route*—In the train—Fontesvilla—Arrival at Beira — A transformation — Lieutenant Hussey-Walsh—Hospitality—The Consul's ball.

SINCE Sister Lucy's serious illness in March 1892, we had escaped the least touch of fever, and, personally, I had enjoyed excellent health. Just, however, as we were congratulating ourselves on our escape, and looking forward to a pleasant journey home, we both fell victims to the malaria demon. We had four attacks, one after the other, and each attack prostrated us both at the same time. There was no one to look after us but a native lad. He sat in a corner of our hut all day; slept on the floor at night; and, having been carefully trained by us as hospital boy, could change our blankets without making us get out of bed, and had some idea of what comfort meant.

Whichever of us had the lower temperature gave the other her medicines, and looked after her as well as was possible. We made the best of the situation, but I must frankly say that it was very uncomfortable, and in my opinion it is not right to leave two women alone in a womanless country. Native women, even, were not available. They never went near a white encampment, though no doubt their prejudice will be overcome as time goes on.

We were both very ill indeed—so ill that we heard afterwards our graves had been dug; but we never could find out whether this was true or not. One night, when we were both at our worst, the doctor sat up all night with us. Sister Lucy was very bad indeed, and threatened with collapse. I had a high temperature even for Africa—106°—and was delirious and saw strange visions. The door of our hut was of the kind called a cottage door, and so made that the lower part could be shut, whilst the upper portion stood half open on account of the heat. Suddenly the door shook violently; a shower of dâgher fell from the walls; it was as if the hut were about to tumble down. Then, on the top of the upper door, something large, black, extraordinary, seemed to appear. The doctor had turned round at the noise, and I, who faced the door, shrieked out that something terrible was coming in!

Dr. Wilson, a big, somewhat slow and phlegmatic Scotchman, jumped across the hut in a most unusual and unprofessional hurry, and banged the door with a violence that shook the whole hut, and appeared most unnecessary. He easily persuaded us that there was nothing near the door; that my delirious fancy had created the monstrous black thing; and that he had only shut the door because the temperature changes towards morning, and sunrise is almost as unhealthy as sunset. But, when we were out of danger, the doctor informed us that a leopard had been wandering about our compound all night; had sprung upon our door; and was gathering itself up to drop into the hut, when he flung the door to, and so shook the creature off, and frightened it away. It consoled itself in the Police Camp with a couple of goats, which it killed and partly devoured. People assured us that the leopard would have been so frightened of us that it would not have done us any harm, but we both agreed in being extremely glad that Dr. Wilson prevented the experiment from being tried.

We found our convalescence very tedious. The natives did their best, and an old white sailor, who had succeeded Charlie, our coolie cook, made great efforts to shine as a professor of invalid cookery. But we could not do justice to his attempts. With the best intentions in the world, and the greatest desire not to be troublesome, it is impossible for sick people to eat unappetising food, roughly prepared and roughly served. We did not therefore recover very fast, and had more than one bad relapse. I do not know how matters would have ended if our friend, Mr. Seymour-Fort, had not come to the rescue. He happened to have with him a Portuguese-speaking native, who had a fair idea of cooking; and every day runners came from Mr. Fort's camp, a distance of four miles, bringing chicken broth, custard puddings, etc. Some of the police, hearing of our difficulty, created a fair imitation of aspic-jelly; it would not have been voted successful in London certainly, but it was quite eatable and pleasant, if a little odd. Pleasanter still was the kind thought which suggested the idea.

Meanwhile Dr. Wilson and the native boys looked after the patients as best they could, but I fear that these were very uncomfortable. Fortunately only slight cases were admitted whilst we were ill, with the exception of one poor man, who was brought in unconscious, and who never recovered consciousness. I was able, in an interval of fever, to attend to him when he was brought in, but twelve hours before he died was obliged to give up and go to bed. I cannot find words to say how miserable it made us both, to lie helpless in our huts, and listen to the moans of the dying man. Again we felt how urgently a third nurse was needed.

We were not quite convalescent when Dr. Wilson was summoned to Beira, where his wife had arrived, and was waiting for him to escort her to Umtali. I had a bad attack of fever shortly after he left, but fortunately Sister Lucy escaped, and was able to look after me and such patients as might be admitted.

One morning after I was convalescent, we were busy arranging a new hut which was being built for the future nurses, and putting a few finishing touches to a rustic porch, which we had added to our sitting-hut, when a smart-looking horseman rode up to the compound. It was the Bishop, riding "Hatfield," the Salisbury steeplechaser. He dismounted, and advanced with out-stretched hands. "Well, you two wonderful people," was his greeting, "I am rejoiced and surprised to see you both alive." We took Dr. Knight Bruce over the little hospital and the huts. He expressed himself as being highly pleased with all the arrangements; declared that he had not expected to find anything so comfortable and civilised; and was rejoiced to think that the incoming nurses would suffer little or no hardships, and could settle down to a three years' spell of work without being discouraged by their surroundings. The Bishop told us that two of his nurses were from University College Hospital, and that he had also engaged two colonial nurses. They were all expected in about a fortnight. He was full of regret for the disorganisation of the Mission, feeling that little had been accomplished since its inauguration two years beforehand. He immediately set about building a brick Mission House, one hundred feet long, and very conveniently arranged. It is situated close to the hospital, on a gentle rise, and commands a lovely view. The building was pushed forward most energetically, and, at the time that this is written, is probably nearly completed.

In about a fortnight after the Bishop's arrival, the waggons bringing up the new nurses reached Umtali. The two English nurses looked like settling down to the work; but one of the Colonial ladies was barely twenty. Both she and her companion might, perhaps, be described in their own phraseology, as "gay cups of tea," and they made no secret of their distaste for their new quarters. They arrived at Umtali on Wednesday, and on the Saturday following left with us for the coast.

The day before our departure a deputation of the townsfolk came up to the hospital, and presented us with an address, signed by between seventy and eighty "representative signatures," as the newspapers say. This demonstration was wholly unexpected, and very touching. Such services as we had been able to render were made far too much of, and we wished we had been able to do more. The township seemed especially pleased at our having started a fund for the erection of a brick hospital, which would no doubt have been nearly finished by this time, but for the Matabele outbreak.

The next day we turned our backs on Umtali, and set out for Beira. The two Colonial nurses travelled in a waggon; Sister Lucy and I were carried in machilas; Dr. Rundell of the Mission, and another white man, went on foot. The waggon could, of course, go no farther than Chimoio, on account of the fly.

Our journey down was most uneventful, except for the fact that Sister Lucy suffered terribly from repeated attacks of fever. She was very plucky about it, and submitted with wonderful patience to being carried along in her machila at a rough trot—which, with a temperature of 105, and aching limbs and head, must have been almost unendurable. It was a red-letter day when we saw the railway embankment winding along through the forest.

The plate-layers' camp was at the forty mile peg. We arrived there late one evening, and the next morning the traffic manager ran us down in trolleys as far as the thirty-five mile peg, where we caught "the down train." Nothing could exceed the excitement of our carriers who had followed so far, pushing the trolleys, when they saw us puffing away in the train. For an incredibly long time they kept up with the train, yelling and bounding over the veldt. We took four of them with us in a truck, and they shook their hands with a disdainful gesture at the friends they left behind.

Arrived at Fontesvilla, the railway terminus on the Pûngwé, we were in doubt where to go, when a Mr. Cathcart, proprietor of a large store, came forward and offered us hospitality. He and his partner turned out of their rooms for us, and did all in their power to make us forget the hardships of the march. We had just missed the river steamer, and had to remain two days in the camp. We met more than one former patient

—amongst them Mr. Holberg, a well-known hunter, who presented us with some pretty tusks. We went boating on the Pûngwé, and renewed our acquaintance with the crocodiles. Sister Lucy picked up a crocodile's egg, which she proposed to bring home. It was a pestiferous egg, and promised to be a regular white elephant, when it was happily broken.

At last the steamer arrived, and early one morning we went on board, and were soon steaming down the Pûngwé. This time there was no question of thirst, hunger, or discomfort. Awnings protected us from the sun, and a tidy luncheon was served.

Our surprise, when we reached Beira, was indeed great. Two years before, it had been simply a flat sandbank, with one or two corrugated iron houses and the tents of the Portuguese soldiers. In 1893 we found streets, stores, and charming houses of the American châlet type. I suppose there are about four hundred inhabitants, the larger number being English. There was a primitive tramway, too, people having their own trucks, and being pushed along by their boys. The streets are still deep in sand, through which it is toilsome to plod one's way. Mr. Hussey-Walsh, the Vice-Consul, offered hospitality to Sister Lucy and myself, the Colonial ladies being accommodated elsewhere.

A large châlet had been provided for the Consul, but it was uninhabitable, being placed on the very edge of the mangrove swamps which make that part of Beira unhealthy. Mr. Hussey-Walsh had, therefore, established himself in a tiny cottage, delightfully situated on the sea shore,—the waves almost dashed into the little verandah on which our bedrooms opened, and the fresh salt smell blew into every corner of the house. Imagine our surprise to find that the Consul's cook and factotum was no other than our Malay boy, Jonosso. He took us under his protection, accompanied us when shopping in the Arab stores, and brought his chief wives to " scrape " to us.

We stayed eleven days with the Consul, and nothing could equal his kindness. He profited by the fact that there were four English-speaking women in Beira, to give a dance on the verandah. There were about ten men to each woman, and to prevent these latter from dying of exhaustion, intervals between the dances were filled up with songs and rousing choruses. Everybody was amused, and the fame of "the Consul's ball" penetrated to the interior of the Dark Continent.

CHAPTER XIV

We leave Beira—On board the German steamer Kaiser—Dar-es-Salaam—Evangelical mission—Mission hospital—Emin Pasha's daughter, Ferida—A madman on board—His strange diet—"We can't lock up an Englishman!"—His death—Zanzibar—The English mission—Splendid organisation—The hospital—On board H.M.S. Raleigh—Bishop Smythies—Aden—The Red Sea—Untimely sausages—Mr. Wolf, the German explorer—Port Said—Europe at last.

DURING the eleven days we spent at Beira we lived in complete uncertainty as to our future plans. No one could tell us what homeward-bound steamer would be the first to arrive. The Union Company's ships run between Cape Town and Beira; whilst the German Company's steamers ply between Natal and Hamburg, touching at Mozambique, Zanzibar, Naples, and other ports. We decided on leaving by the first steamer that put in, and on the 27th of June we saw the German steamer *Kaiser* steaming into the bay. Early the next morning the Consul and one or two other friends took us on board the *Kaiser*, a large and fairly comfortable ship, the saloon and cabins being on the main deck and, therefore, much less stuffy than those on the ordinary Atlantic steamer.

Our good-byes being said we set out for Mozambique, the first port at which we were to touch. We had seen Mozambique two years before, and knew every inch of the town, and, therefore, were not much interested in our journey until we arrived at Dar-es-Salaam. This German settlement greatly surprised us. The *Kaiser* rounded a rocky island, and, steaming along a narrow channel, suddenly entered a land-locked bay round which Dar-es-Salaam is built. Had it not been for the groves of cocoanut palms, one might have imagined oneself at Gmünden or Baden. Large white stone houses, two or three stories high, with brown wooden balconies running round them, are an unusual sight anywhere in Africa. The place seemed astonishingly flourishing, and we wondered we had not heard more about it, as it looked a far more important place than Beira. On inquiry, however, we discovered that the buildings were not the outcome of individual enterprise as at Beira, but were nearly all built by the Government. The inhabitants too were mostly officials.

Wishing to visit the Mission Hospital, we asked our way of a magnificent personage whose white uniform was resplendent with gold buttons and braid. We thought he must be a General at least, but discovered that he was only a post-office clerk. He directed us to the hospital and mission house belonging to the German Evangelical Mission. Large and well-cultivated grounds surrounded the hospital, and afforded work to a number of natives whose picturesque locations, scattered here and there, were beautifully kept. An elderly deaconess received us very amiably, and took us over the hospital. She told us that the nursing work was entirely done by Brothers, she and the other deaconess having nothing to do with the sick, but being altogether employed in cooking and keeping house. In the rare case of a woman being admitted to hospital they nursed her. The wards were large and very clean; but they looked comfortless, and seemed to be recklessly ventilated, a small hurricane blowing through them flapping the coverings of the beds and beating directly on the patients' heads. Kind as the nursing Brothers seemed, we both felt that we should have been very sorry to know that any one we cared for was in the Dar-es-Salaam Hospital.

We were struck by the absence of any interest, outside their own work, shown by the Deaconesses and the Brothers. They had never heard of Mashonaland, of hospitals at Cape Town and Kimberley, and they did not even know that there was a large English mission close by at Zanzibar. They had heard of Roman Catholic missions, and appeared to think that all the hospital work in the world was either done by them or by their own Evangelical Mission. They gave us excellent coffee and cake, despatching us back to our ship with many good wishes.

As we strolled back to the landing-place we met the " Governor's lady," as she is generally called, a fair-haired German in a startling toilette, with some unusually fair, fat children. Amongst these a melancholy-looking coloured child attracted our attention. We were told that this was Ferida, daughter of Emin Pasha. She came on board that evening in charge of Sister Marie of the German Red Cross Sisterhood, who was to take her to Berlin, and place her under the care of her father's sister. Ferida was a wizened-looking child of about eight or nine, only redeemed from positive ugliness by a pair of magnificent Eastern eyes—large, lustrous, and solemn. She understood and spoke a little German, French, and Italian; but said little or nothing, made no noise, and moped about in corners.

We had another interesting traveller on board, in the shape of a madman. This unfortunate was shipped on board the *Kaiser*, at Durban I think, and soon proved very troublesome. He wandered all over the ship; chiefly frequenting the cabins of the second-class passengers, amongst whom he travelled. He ate the soap, drank hair-wash and eau de cologne, used the tooth-brushes, and picked up any stray coins he could find. Every now and then he was searched and his unlawful acquisitions taken away from him. When we asked why he was not shut up in a cabin and taken out under supervision, we were much amused at being told that it was because he was an Englishman. "If he were German," said the Captain, "I would lock him up; but he is a bold man who locks up an Englishman." The poor madman never reached home; between the diet of soap and hair-wash, and the heat of the Red Sea, his health gave way. He had an apoplectic seizure, and died without recovering consciousness.

Zanzibar was the first really oriental-looking place we had ever seen, and we revelled in the narrow streets; the shops full of picturesque rubbish; the open sheds where we could watch the silver-workers hammering out designs on quaintly-shaped cups, bangles, and anklets. We fell easy victims to the embroidery-sellers and moonstone merchants who thronged the ship, and who began by asking £20, and ended by gratefully accepting 10s. for the same goods.

Of course we were curious to see the English Mission Hospital, having heard a great deal about it, and being much interested in it. The English Church, or Cathedral as I think it is called, surprised us by its size and beauty. It is large and finely proportioned, built of white stone, and stands in the midst of a group of graceful cocoa-nut palms. The Bishop was holding a synod in the church as we looked in, and a clergyman, kneeling near the entrance, who proved to be the Chaplain of H.M.S. *Raleigh*, rose from his place, and conducted us to the neighbouring Mission House. Here we were received by a charming old lady, who manages the house, and looks after the wellbeing of Bishop and clergy. She was having tea prepared for the Synod, and proposed taking us across to the hospital, requesting us to return to tea. To this we gladly assented, and, following our guide, crossed a small open space leading to the hospital. Ascending a short flight of steps we found ourselves in a delightfully cool recess—half room, half loggia—and here we saw a convalescent mission-worker lying on a comfortable sofa, whilst another was embroidering at a small table. It was a cosy and homelike scene.

One of the nurses, in a fresh white uniform, then appeared, and took us over the building. We admired the comfortably furnished rooms provided for Europeans, and the nurses' pretty bedrooms, each opening on a broad balcony. We then visited the beautifully-ordered native wards; the large, well-supplied dispensary; the spotless kitchens; and were delighted with the air of orderly activity which prevailed in every department. The nurses looked fagged. They told us that the work was happily rather slack just then; one of the four had fever, and the work had been exceptionally heavy for the other three. But, though looking a little worn and weary, they were very bright and cheery, and evidently thoroughly content with their work and surroundings.

We carried away a very pleasant impression of our visit, and went back to the Mission House, where we found a number of clergy at tea. We were rather disappointed to find that the Bishop, feeling very tired, had retired to his room. During the meal we heard a great deal about the Mission, its schools and industrial settlements; and it was delightful to note the earnestness of our entertainers, and their complete trust in the Bishop.

We met Bishop Smythies the next day

on board H.M.S. *Raleigh*. Admiral Bedford had given us tea, and shown us some native curios, and, as we said goodbye to him, we met the Bishop, who had been entertained by the Chaplain. He was exceedingly kind to us, and said many encouraging things about our work up country, which seemed familiar to him. We fully appreciated the charm of his grave and dignified manner, and easily understood the sentiments of veneration and personal devotion to him with which all his workers are inspired. On all sides we heard of the splendid work which the Zanzibar Mission is accomplishing, and of its admirable organisation. Mr. Eugen Wolf, the German explorer, who joined the *Kaiser* at Zanzibar, told us that he had seen most of the various Missions which are scattered over Africa, and that he considered the Mission over which Bishop Smythies presided to be the only one which stood on an equal footing with the Roman Catholic Missions.

From Zanzibar to Aden the journey was

uneventful and monotonous. Most of the other passengers knew the east coast well, but Sister Lucy and I were childishly delighted with the Aden camel market and all the odd figures riding about on camels. We had only a few hours in which to amuse ourselves with these strange sights before the *Kaiser* set off again, and steamed away into the dreaded Red Sea. It was hotter in the Red Sea than any one belonging the ship had ever known it to be. One lived night and day in a sort of Turkish bath, there were no punkahs in the saloon, and I must say the food was hardly in keeping with the state of the atmosphere. I remember one stifling day the Captain, as he sat down to luncheon, announced that the glass was at 110° in the saloon. Immediately afterwards an enormous dish of steaming sausages and sauerkraut was handed round, and some of the ship's officers actually helped themselves largely. Most of the English fled in despair, and collapsed on their deck chairs in a limper condition than before. It was at Aden that we heard of the loss of the *Victoria;* and the Germans on board, some of whom were naval officers, spent their after-dinner leisure during the rest of the journey in manœuvring imaginary fleets, made of little balls of bread, and explaining what the English officers ought to have done and didn't do.

The only person of resource on board was Mr. Eugen Wolf, whom I have mentioned before. He had just returned from Uganda, from whence he had made a record march to the coast. We could not get him to talk about the Uganda question, however. All he would say was that Sir G. Portal was a "splendid fellow." Mr. Wolf is a brilliant linguist, and spoke English remarkably well. He was more at home on board the *Kaiser* than the Captain, and whenever anything unusual was required, or anyone wanted help or advice, "Go to Mr. Wolf," was the cry. This tireless wanderer has bought a charming retreat at Taormina, and there he says he intends to settle down and end his days; but at present he is far from the "settling-down" period, and very likely is even now starting off for the uttermost end of the earth.

We steamed very slowly through the Suez Canal, and arrived late one evening at Port Said. We were to spend the night here coaling, so with one accord we all went on shore, the town being brightly lit up, and thronged with people.

Here we possessed ourselves of some of the gold embroidery for which Port Said is famous, and ran in and out of the curious concert rooms and dancing halls which abound. The doctor of the *Kaiser* accompanied us on this tour of inspection, and generally swept us out of these odd places of amusement almost as soon as we had entered them. I suppose a great deal of fighting goes on in them. The dancing halls seemed very dull. The audience sat drinking beer at little tables, whilst women in long flowing draperies glided about on a raised platform waving their arms, and looking like so many sleep-walkers.

We left Port Said early the next morning, and after a four days' journey cast anchor at Naples.

Those who have followed us in our wanderings can easily imagine with what joy and emotion we found ourselves once more in Europe. We both felt that we had hardly deserved such good fortune, and vowed that we would never leave it again. The Arabs, however, have a proverb which says: "He who has tasted of African water, must return to drink of it once more"; and certainly there is a penetrating charm about the "Dark Continent" which must be felt, but cannot be described. So, in spite of all the joy of return, the warmth of home comfort, the pleasure of familiar ways, I cannot feel at all certain that either of us has looked her last upon the Southern Cross.

THE END

Printed by R. & R. CLARK, *Edinburgh.*

www.ingramcontent.com/pod-product-compliance
Lightning Source LLC
Chambersburg PA
CBHW030255240426
43673CB00040B/981